Another Look at Women's Education

Edited by ROBERT M. GAY

Another

SIMMONS COLLEGE

Introduction by GEORGE D. STODDARD

Bancroft

Beatley

Look at Women's Education

and other

essays and addresses

BOSTON   Nineteen hundred fifty-five

Designer: VIRGINIA L. BRATTON

Preface

BANCROFT BEATLEY RETIRES AFTER
*twenty-two years of devoted service to the College. His
decision to do so was wise from his point of view, for
he is young enough to look forward to a happy and
profitable leisure; and his colleagues, while regretting his
resignation, cannot of course begrudge him his freedom.
We can only thank him for his wise and fruitful administration, and wish him every happiness in the future.*

*We can add nothing to Dr. Stoddard's warm tribute;
but we have felt that Mr. Beatley (as he prefers to be
called) has contributed much to the Simmons tradition,
as well as to the conception of women's education in
general, that deserves a lasting memorial. This book is
the result.*

*It consists of articles, essays, and addresses prepared
over the entire period of his tenure, from his installation
as President in 1933 to the present.*

*Since it was inevitable that papers dealing with the
same main subject should show repetition of idea and
expression, it was part of my task as Editor to exercise
the prerogative of selection and excision; and this I
have done, as indeed he asked me to do. But I have not
altered the text, except where there were obvious mistakes in transcription.*

*In sum the book has the unity of one man's views re-
garding the higher education of women; but it sees such
education in broadest perspective, as having a fourfold*

530

purpose of preparing women for life in the family, in society, in a profession, and in personal and private enrichment. It is natural that, Simmons being a professional college, much space should be given to the third of these aspects, especially because of a popular tendency to confuse professional preparation with mere training in skills — a confusion that has sometimes led to a misapprehension of the kind of education the College offers.

While working over the contents I was reminded of a fact I had often before noted, that the curricular pattern of Simmons is puzzling to many, because of the double division into departments and schools. Most people associate "department" with college and "school" with university; and questions sometimes asked suggest that some are not clear about what the terms mean here. In briefest statement "department" refers to a division of general knowledge and "school" to a specialization in professional techniques, the departments being open to all students, while the schools are confined to those preparing for a specific vocation; so we speak of Departments of English, History, Physics, Psychology, etc., and Schools of Science, Publication, Nursing, Business, etc. But all students — at least all working for the degree — combine in their individual curricula the general studies of the departments with the specialized studies of the schools. This pattern is in fact intrinsic in the Simmons plan of education and in adopting it half a century ago the College was a pioneer.

I have thought it of value to explain our organization, because it suggests so vividly the attempt of the College to find a balance and reciprocation between savoir and savoir-faire, in the belief that all sound professional education must rest on a foundation of general knowledge.

THE EDITOR

April, 1955

Contents

Introduction

THE SIMMONS PLAN OFFERS A *good defense against the unconscious arrogance of the unprepared person. Dilettantism is uncomfortable in the presence of some degree of mastery in a particular field. At Simmons College general education is not undertaken in a vacuum; it is wrapped around a hard-core specialization. There is room for both kinds of intellectual enrichment.*

In the past some colleges for women, eager to display the mental ability of their students, have ignored the special interests of women. Eighty per cent of American women marry and become homemakers, on a full-time or part-time basis. It is unrealistic to expect most men, fully engaged in other occupations, to carry the main burden of work and child rearing in the home. It is equally unrealistic to hold that a college program for women should ignore the home or out-of-home occupations of women.

The days of the apprentice are numbered. The occupations long preferred by women — teaching and nursing and business, library and sociological work — now require substantial academic preparation. Moreover, there has been erected upon such occupations a superstructure of vast importance. We have not only nurses, secretaries, and technicians who know the meaning of the college experience, which is, after all, simply to keep on learning. We have also increasing numbers of women doctors, lawyers, professors and scientists, and leaders in government, business, and community affairs.

Look about when anything of importance is coming up — anything affecting education, art or humane services. When the Babbitts and the Helen Hokinson ladies are canceled out, the remainder will favor the women! We know why. The woman with a well-rounded education that combines the liberal, the vocational, and the homemaking arts puts more of her education to work where it counts. The man, deep in the financial or sports page, talks knowingly about community life. The woman epitomizes community life. She likes people, not percentages.

Simmons College — led by two men, Henry Lefavour and Bancroft Beatley, both following the early vision of John Simmons — has been fortunate. It was not at any time a trade school. It was never just another women's college. It offered a balanced educational program.

It is easy to see from his writings that Mr. Beatley was not a man to be satisfied with generalities. He called for a fresh look at women's education. It was no strain for him, or anyone, to discover that "the fundamental objectives of education at the college level concern the development of abilities and attitudes that will function in the intellectual, aesthetic, social, and practical life of the individual." The question was, What kind of curriculum, what kind of college, would best contribute to this idea of a well-rounded personality? To get down to cases, What problems would Simmons graduates have to meet? Beatley placed them in four categories:

1. Home and family life
2. The community
3. Occupational life
4. The personal, inner life of the individual.

Then, without rancor, he proceeded to measure the standard liberal arts colleges for women in terms of these criteria — and found them wanting. They emphasized, for the most part, the inner, or intellectual, life. For all *this concentration, only a few graduates developed any mastery of the humane disciplines. Away from home and community, with few well-defined occupational objectives, the young women showed no special liking for the fragmented offerings in the liberal arts which had been transferred — bag and baggage — from men's colleges that were on the verge of trying something different. The women did demonstrate that they could equal the men in reciting classroom lessons.*

In short, women's intuition was sound — they had a right to be bored. They were being bored by experts who knew the women's weakness at this time of struggle for equal rights. In those days, any complaint, any default, would have wagged the heads of the knowing males: "A woman can't learn these things; her place is in the home, the school, or the unskilled labor market."

Occasionally the graduates of a traditional women's college would enter the same occupation as the Simmons girl. The point is, they seemed perpetually unprepared to do so. As Beatley observed, the traditional college has been "something less than liberal in its attitude toward education for occupational life." Many would stay at home for a while, but the majority went straight to their objective — the man, the home, the small-family life. It was a good objective, too, but as unrelated as possible to anything found in the curriculum.

Presently the distance between the various types of women's colleges is narrowing. Homemaking and a prior or concurrent career are often consistent. The career tests powers not tested in classroom performance. It calls for the organization of abilities. It sorts out learning, as it were, and surely it sorts out people. To prepare in college for this desirable use of abilities is a matter of common sense. It was only a prejudiced view of women's work and of their activities in home, community, and nation, coupled with strange ideas on the nature of children, that rejected this early "common sense." All pioneers in women's education had to en-

dure contempt — the subject was always "good for a laugh." But the men who laughed so easily at the "Bloomer Girls" would have to think up another response to the latest bathing-suit styles.

This is not to say that the Simmons graduate is essentially a radical. Doubtless she is back of many a reform in office, home, clinic, or community, but it is the kind of reform that springs from "know-how" and the sharing of responsibility. It is reform from within the occupation or service, and it sticks.

In all this the liberal arts help. They are, indeed, a form of studying and knowing that permits the Simmons graduate, like any other, to join in the elite company of those who think and compare and create. It is refreshing to read Mr. Beatley on this question which has proved baffling to many:

"No one would question the value of the presence in our society of hosts of women who are widely read, who possess a discriminating taste in the fine arts and music, who are deeply religious, and who have worked out for themselves a satisfying philosophy of life. Such women have insights that make them interesting people to know, and they possess the inner resources which *may* enable them to live happily with themselves. I say '*may* enable them to live happily with themselves' advisedly, for unless these women also have made satisfactory adjustments to home and family life, unless they have solved the problem of financial support, and unless they are making their lives count in some way for the common good, they will not be happy people."

Well, let's have more happy people! *It is a concept deeply rooted in the human race and explored by philosophers and social scientists since the time of the early Greeks. It is no surface phenomenon, no Pollyanna trick — not in our days of anxiety — of a disaster-sense that is bone-deep. We who are about to die will leave no one to receive the grand salute. As we look ahead, in war or peace, the personal arts in which women excel loom large. They are a saving grace.*

Now it is one thing to have ideas on the education of women — every parent, teacher, or child has something to say on the subject. It is quite another thing to be responsible for their evaluation and execution. Bancroft Beatley's truly great contribution lies precisely there. The new Simmons brought about in the twenty-two years of his presidency is the "lengthened shadow" of this man.

He has steadily maintained the basic idea of combining the vocational-professional and the liberal disciplines into an integrated program. Through temperament, training, and educational conviction, he has given stout support to the Simmons program in general education as the essential correlate to the technical studies.

He has diligently explored new opportunities for women — "in science and industry, business, retailing, publishing, library science, home economics, nursing, and social work."

He has emphasized good teaching, patiently searching out the best talent. That he has kept the student herself at the heart of the program is shown by the many improvements in admission practices, guidance, health, and placement.

With regard to plant and facilities — the pictures tell the story — see the five handsome new buildings, together with plant improvements everywhere.

Most impressive, too, are Mr. Beatley's achievements in community relations. He has made the metropolitan area of Boston his home grounds, turning naturally to the leaders of this great community, and they to him. Any Congressional committee investigating Simmons will find the college interlocked with the directorates (and the enthusiasms) of dozens of city enterprises — with hospitals, clinics, business and industrial plants, libraries, welfare and civic agencies! Is that bad?

Nobody knows better than Mr. Beatley that there is still more to be done. Endowments are needed, especially the free funds that permit income to be used where needed. Scholarships will help. This is no time for the alumnae to lean back, feeling easy and complacent under well-deserved praise. To look backward for long is not in the tradition *of Simmons College, and I use the word advisedly. Simmons was one of the first colleges to embark wholeheartedly on a combined think-and-prepare plan. Other women's colleges will date their acceptance of this idea, and their zealous support of it, much later than 1902 — perhaps as late as the year 2000!*

In the meantime, the College of Simmons and Lefavour and Beatley moves ahead, secure in the loyalty of faculty and student body and of its thousands of graduates and friends the world over.

GEORGE D. STODDARD

Part one

Another Look at Women's Education

WOMEN'S EDUCATION IS BEING viewed critically today as never before. During World War II, colleges that had never acknowledged a vocational objective inaugurated schools of nursing, offered courses in map-making for the War Department, and undertook to educate women in a wide variety of technical subjects, to help meet the shortage of trained personnel. Women students, impatient with exclusively liberal arts programs, sought increasingly to plan their courses so that they would be prepared to do something upon graduation.

In the recent discussions of general education, moreover, the probable uses to which education will be put have played a prominent part.

WHAT IS THE BEST CURRICULUM?

In September, 1949, *Fortune* published a survey of higher education. In this study, laymen were asked to judge the relative importance of ten suggested objectives of higher education, first as applied to men, and then to women. In the case of men's education, "training for a particular occupation or profession" and "a better chance to get ahead in the world" rated high in importance; while "preparation for marriage and family life" and "a better appreciation of such things as literature, art, and music" rated low. On the other hand,

3

"preparation for marriage and family life" was of first importance for women's education; while "desire and ability to be a more useful citizen" and "a broader knowledge of the world and world problems" received relatively low ratings.

This poll reveals a widespread opinion that women's education should seek, in some respects at least, different goals from that of men.

There will be a general agreement to the proposition that the best curriculum is one that recognizes and anticipates the kind of problems most graduates will have to meet. These problems are found in four areas:

1. The personal life of the individual
2. Life in the community
3. Home and family life
4. Occupational life.

I believe that we should think in terms of developing the attitudes and abilities which will enable our students to function effectively in *all* these areas. Insofar as the potential contributions of women to our common life differ from those of men, our curriculum must acknowledge these differences and provide accordingly. At the same time it must recognize the need for the greatest flexibility in providing for individual variations in personal goals of men and women and their capacities to achieve these goals.

THE PERSONAL LIFE OF THE INDIVIDUAL

If we examine the *traditional* pattern of women's education in the light of the foregoing, we find that its primary concern has been the developing of abilities and attitudes calculated to enrich the personal and inner life of the student.

No one would question the value of the presence in our society of hosts of women who are widely read, who possess a discriminating taste in the fine arts and music, who are deeply religious, and who have worked out for themselves a satisfying philosophy of life. Such women have insights that make them interesting people to know, and they possess the inner resources which may enable them to live happily with themselves. But unless these women also have made satisfactory adjustments to home and family life, unless they have solved the problem of financial support, and unless they are making their lives count in some way for the common good, they will not be happy people.

Women's education has already achieved its largest measure of success in enriching the personal life of the individual. Though the emphasis in women's education may be shifted so as to bring other objectives into greater prominence than they now possess, there is no thought here that what is commonly called culture is no longer important. It is of vital importance, but not to the extent of excluding other objectives.

Life in the Community

To a lesser extent the traditional pattern of women's education has contributed to the student's understanding of man and the social order.

Until recently, the languages, literature, and the fine arts have been favorite fields for women students. Today an analysis of their major studies would reveal a strong shift of interest toward psychology and sociology as well as the older social sciences — history, government, and economics.

Whether this will result in a higher level of civic behavior is open to question. Granted that knowledge is power, knowledge of itself will not produce action. There must be both the knowledge of how to act and the desire for such action. Though some college women have thrown themselves wholeheartedly into such intelligent programs as that of the League of Women Voters, the proportion is all too low. As a result, college women have been far less influential in civic affairs than might properly be expected from the superior education in social understanding which they have enjoyed.

The problem of women's education in producing graduates with a strong civic conscience is not to be met simply by offering more courses in the social sciences or by increasing the required exposure to such courses. A more fruitful approach is to be sought by evaluating the desirable functions of civic life, and by selecting the subject matter best calculated to produce better civic behavior. It must be admitted that we do not yet know how to produce this result either in the colleges or in the lower schools, but extensive research now in progress promises a better solution to the problem than any we have yet achieved.

HOME AND FAMILY LIFE

If we turn to the objective of home and family life, we note an amazing unwillingness on the part of traditional women's education to face the obvious fact that the typical college woman looks forward to marriage, a home of her own, and children.

To be sure, most colleges offer to women the opportunity to study child psychology, and an increasing number provide courses on marriage, though the latter are frequently regarded as extracurricular and not quite reputable. But the systematic preparation of young women for a function which we can be certain will characterize the lives of most of them has been signally ignored.

One of the most obvious improvements needed in women's education today is the offering of instruction in homemaking, at least to the extent of home management and child guidance, in all colleges attended by women, and the encouragement of all women students to include in their programs some experience in this area.

Work Is Dominant Life Interest

The objectives of vocational education have traditionally been held incompatible with the demands of liberal education. But for many years liberal arts colleges have been a major source for the recruiting of teachers, especially for secondary schools, and more women graduates have entered teaching directly from college than have sought any other profession. As the requirements for teaching have become more and more professionalized, these colleges have established departments of education for the purpose of furnishing the necessary technical training.

And yet there has been no wholehearted acceptance of the professional objective by many of the colleges educating women. Why this is so, is hard to understand. To be sure, there has been more than a suggestion that because vocational education deals with practical outcomes it is unworthy of a place in the liberal curriculum.

We are all familiar with the cliché that education is not preparation for earning a living, but preparation for life — as if it were possible to separate the two. For most of us, work is a dominant life interest, and a theory of education which studiously ignores that fact appears to be something less than liberal.

To me, there is no opposition between the aims of liberal education on the one hand and vocational education on the other. General education — to use the more comprehensive term — must contribute to all four of the areas in which our graduates are expected to function. As occupational life is one of these areas, vocational education is an essential phase of general education.

When *Time* magazine recently asked women graduates what they wished they might have got in college, a large proportion replied, "More specific training for occupations." We find this same need recognized in the replies to the American Association of University Women 1948 Questionnaire on Higher Education.

PREPARATION FOR EARNING A LIVELIHOOD

If we talk with the deans of women in our colleges of arts and sciences, we discover that students are trying to put together programs that will prepare them for some congenial employment. These young women are approaching the program of arts and sciences with a strong economic motive, and they are arranging as best they can to satisfy their needs for education toward self-support.

In this matter of professional education men and women are in different positions. Many college men, preparing for a lifetime of employment, plan to take their professional education in graduate school. For most women, however, vocational objectives are related to an ultimate goal of marriage, home, and children. Accordingly, though some women will quite properly seek careers in professions requiring extensive graduate study, the great majority must be served vocationally in college or not at all.

We at Simmons find that the occupations that interest college women and challenge their abilities are most commonly those involving work in which there is both an intellectual content and a concern for people — work in churches, schools, libraries, social agencies, health agencies, and business establishments.

For occupations of this type, the opportunities available to women graduates without technical education have steadily declined, and the amount of technical education demanded has steadily increased. Consider the months and sometimes years which now must go into the college training of a public health nurse, a nutritionist, a textile analyst, a medical technologist, a legal secretary, a personnel worker, a school librarian, an editorial assistant, a physical therapist — to mention only a few occupations now being entered by college women who have the requisite technical education.

CAREERS VERSUS MARRIAGE

The ideal program of occupational education for college women is one which acknowledges the dual objectives of job and marriage. It is not easy to plan such a program, because of wide variations in the relationship between employment and marriage exhibited in the lives of individual women graduates. Some college women are definitely career-minded. Of these, some will make a clear choice of career over marriage, and others will combine career with marriage.

The largest group of college women today, however, comprises those who seek a satisfying means of self-support between graduation and marriage. They have no thought of entering upon a long-range career. Perhaps when their children have grown to the point where they no longer require constant attention, these women may wish to return to the employment for which they were trained, in order to make their lives count — or circumstances may force them to do so. This group of women look upon homemaking as their main occupation and regard employment as a secondary interest.

It is impossible to predict which pattern an individual undergraduate is going to follow. Experience has shown that some of our most ardently career-minded undergraduates exercise the womanly prerogative of changing their minds when the right man comes along, and others who expected to marry shortly after graduation find themselves in lifelong careers.

BOTH SKILL AND INTELLIGENCE

The pattern of education which will serve both groups has been found to be one which combines technical skill and technical intelligence. The former is essential to placement and initial success for both the career-minded and those who expect to work for only a brief period. The latter is primary in importance for those entering a career.

Many misinformed persons think of technical education as synonymous with training in skills. Though some marketable skill must result from vocational education, the higher the occupational level the more the training must emphasize technical intelligence.

Since the occupations which college women will seek to enter are professional, or at least semiprofessional, there is a large body of facts, ideas, and principles on which successful work in these occupations depends. Technical intelligence is the *what* and the *why,* rather than the *how;* and as I have said in the following article, all the skill in the world in the preparation of food will not make a sound nutritionist.

Skills are an essential and worthy part of job preparation, but we must relate them constantly to the fundamental ideas and principles which constitute technical intelligence. If we do so, we can be confident that our graduates will qualify initially for positions in fields which challenge their abilities, and that they will have the basis for progressive growth toward positions of larger responsibility commanding their best efforts.

CONTRIBUTION TO HOMEMAKING

On the other hand, it is fortunate that the professional areas which interest women most have large carry-over values for the home. The field of professional home economics is perhaps the best case in point, but teaching, nursing, librarianship, social work, and many phases of business all provide opportunities for developing understanding and abilities that are of value also in homemaking. To the extent that there is similarity in content between the experiences involved in professional training and the activities of the home, the waste of time and energy by those who leave professional work for marriage may be more seeming than real.

TO CREATE A UNIFIED PROGRAM

These, it seems to me, are some of the considerations that education must take into account to insure that women graduates will be capable of functioning effectively in life after college. It is the burden of this discussion that women's education must attempt to synthesize personal development, social-civic education, preparation for home and family life, and vocational education.

Though for the purposes of our thinking it has been helpful to consider the abilities and attitudes in these four phases of women's education as relatively independent, we shall not fully serve the educational needs of college women until we have woven these components into the fabric of a unified personality capable of coping with life in all its aspects.

Mary Jones Goes To College

THE YEAR 1937 WAS A SIGNIFI-
cant year in the history of American education. It
marked the completion of the first hundred years of
higher education for women. When Mary Lyon founded
the seminary which later became Mount Holyoke College, and Oberlin College first admitted women students, there were sixty colleges for men in this country,
but not a single college for women. Today, when men
and women attend college in nearly equal numbers, it is
hard for us to imagine an earlier period when women
were denied the opportunity. Someone has said of life
that the first hundred years are the hardest. However
applicable this comment to human beings, it is obviously true of institutions. The history of the last
century shows women struggling for recognition in the
political and economic world. The founding of colleges
for women was only one aspect of that struggle. In a
world dominated by men, women had first to demonstrate the falsity of the notion that they were intellectually inferior. It was natural, then, that our first efforts
in the college education for women were directed toward
showing that women could compete successfully with
men in a program designed for men. In fact, one college, Bryn Mawr, in its efforts to prove the point, maintained standards which were intellectually more severe

than those of any men's college. As the typical college for men in this country at that time was the so-called liberal arts college, this pattern was adopted for nearly all the women's colleges established in the latter half of the nineteenth century.

As I take it, the liberal arts college believes that the best preparation for living is widening the intellectual horizon and disciplining the mind and will, without attempting to prepare the student for any particular career. The practical effect of this program for young women who had to use their education in earning a living was to turn them in the direction of teaching, the only occupation for which the liberal arts program seemed to provide preparation. Until rather recently there has not been much place in the American college for the girl who knew she would have to go to work, but who didn't want to teach.

Colleges like Simmons are set up to serve just such young women. They believe that general education and professional education, within the same institution, are entirely compatible.

Let's take the case of Mary Jones. Mary comes from an average home where her parents have had the common American ideal of sending their children to college. The resources of the Jones family will not permit Mary to spend more than four years in higher education. After her college days are over, she will have to be on her own. She has done well in high school, she likes school work, and she likes a good time. Some day she expects to marry and have a home of her own. But she knows that she won't marry just for the sake of it. She would like to prove to herself first that she can do a job well, even though she doesn't plan to make a career of it. In any case, she will have to earn her living between the time she leaves college and the time she

13

marries. And there are thousands of Mary Joneses in this country.

I believe that the college which best serves Mary Jones is the one which looks forward and sees the kind of life she is likely to live. In the first place, Mary should become an intelligent adult. As a member of the community she should have an active interest in social, political, and economic problems. Although it is, perhaps, too much to expect Mary or anyone else fully to understand these problems in all their complexity, she should have an eager interest in them, an open-minded attitude, and a foundation for increased understanding.

Then Mary needs to develop her understanding of people, how they react to one another and to her. She needs to have resources for enriching her life, through literature, art, music, and worthwhile recreations. If she marries and has a family, she will necessarily devote a large share of her time to managing her home and guiding the development of her children — to say nothing of her husband. In all these respects the College can help Mary to become a cultivated woman with broad interests and a satisfying philosophy of life.

But this is not enough. We must face the realities of the situation. Mary must find a job — not just any old job — but one which really challenges her abilities. If the College makes no attempt to prepare her to enter employment, she will probably have to take special courses after graduation to fit her for work. And this isn't fair to Mary, who has exhausted her economic resources in completing the four-year course. Some of the liberal arts colleges are recognizing this difficulty and are providing a few practical courses which may be taken as additional work without credit toward the degree. This is all right as far as it goes, but it falls far short of meeting the demands of the situation.

To my mind, the program of the typical college for women in America is a luxury program. It is well suited to the young woman who is able to continue her education in a professional school after graduating from college or to one who for any of a number of reasons is not concerned with earning her living. It may also serve to some extent the girl who plans to enter teaching, though this field increasingly insists upon preparation in a graduate professional school. For the Mary Joneses, a college which combines liberal education and vocational preparation is essential.

In all the controversy that has raged over introducing vocational courses into an academic program, one thing stands out in my mind. The opponents of the idea seem to base their argument on the premise that liberal education is one thing and vocational education something quite different and perhaps unworthy. This seems to me to be due either to a narrow conception of liberal education or to a lack of understanding of vocational education, or both. One commonly hears the view expressed that the college is designed not to teach young people to earn a living, but to live — as if it were possible to separate the two. For most of us, work is a dominant life interest, and a type of education which studiously ignores this fact appears to be something less than liberal.

If the critics of vocational education in the college think of it as exclusively a training in skills, I can readily sympathize with their objection, but I cannot agree with their conception of the field. We at Simmons believe that in preparing our students for occupational life, we must first provide a firm foundation of occupational intelligence. We do not ignore training in skills as unworthy, because some skill is essential if the graduate is to secure a position and be successful in her first work.

What is this professional intelligence which we regard as all-important? It is the body of ideas and principles upon which the work of the field is based. It is the *what* and the *why,* rather than the *how.* All the skill in the world in the preparation of food will not make a sound nutritionist. She must be first of all a competent student of dietetics. Dietetics, in turn, is an organized body of subject matter drawing its materials from chemistry, physiology, pathology, physics, economics, sociology, and psychology — all thoroughly respectable members of the academic hierarchy. Because this subject matter is selected to serve the needs of a particular occupational group, does it change its basic character and cease to be an intellectual discipline? That technical courses of this type may in some cases be superficial and fail to challenge the intellectual powers of the students is unfortunately true, but it is also a fact that courses in the history of literature are sometimes little more than an enumeration of men and of dates. President Neilson of Smith College has recently said that a teacher can start from any point and gradually work through the whole range of human knowledge. If this be true, then courses which aim to develop professional intelligence are not fundamentally different from liberal courses. They merely use a different point of departure.

Now let's see how all this works out for Mary Jones. As I have said, she has a good mind, the desire for a college education, and the need to go to work immediately on graduation from college. As yet she does not know whether she will embark upon a career, or work for a few years prior to marriage. She has no very strong vocational preference, but thinks she would like to do secretarial work. Let us assume that she selects Simmons College because of the opportunity to combine liberal education and professional preparation. Before accepting her as a student, the College inquires carefully into her previous preparation, her aptitude for college work, and her social and personal characteristics. The latter are important considerations for all colleges, but especially so in a college like Simmons because of the difficulty of securing positions for graduates who exhibit major personality defects.

Mary selects her program for the first year under the guidance of her faculty adviser, who is provided with a wide range of information concerning her family background, her health, her previous education, and her interests and attitudes as shown by numerous tests taken almost immediately upon her arrival. The courses which she decides upon are similar to those offered in the liberal arts college: English, a foreign language, a course in social studies or history, and one in science. The selection has no necessary relation to Mary's desire to become a secretary. Rather, this first year gives her the opportunity to learn more concerning the careers open to educated women. Her decision to be a secretary is regarded as tentative, to be confirmed or modified by her better understanding of her own interests and abilities and by a knowledge of the varied programs which the College offers: programs leading to positions in business offices, stores, publishing houses, offices, laboratories, schools, hospitals, and social agencies. Toward the close of her first year Mary elects to enter one of the eight professional divisions or schools of the College. Previous experience indicates that the chances are four out of five that she will be confirmed in her original choice, in which case she will enter the School of Business and will henceforth be guided in her entire program by the Director of that School.

The work of the remaining three years is divided between general and specialized courses, the emphasis on the latter increasing as Mary approaches graduation. The specialized courses develop her business intelligence and competence in the techniques which she will employ as a secretary. I use the term "business intelligence" to include that body of ideas and principles which makes business activities meaningful. To acquire this under- standing, Mary will have the opportunity to take courses in business economics, business law, business organiza- tion, statistics, finance, marketing, and personnel. The content of these courses is in turn selected from the fields of economics and the other social sciences, from mathematics, and from psychology. At the same time Mary will be acquiring an adequate skill in shorthand and typewriting, and a familiarity with the various types of office machines. Finally, in her senior year, she will spend a limited amount of time in "practice work," in the field, gaining experience in actual working condi- tions in an office.

Her preoccupation with professional preparation dur- ing these years, however, will not lead her to ignore the cultural side of her education. On the contrary, she will find time to continue her study of history, art, music, literature, or such other subjects as interest her.

In selecting a case for illustration, I have purposely chosen one in which the amount of skill-training is high as compared with most of the fields for which the Col- lege offers preparation. And yet when we sum up the college education of Mary Jones we find that she has devoted the equivalent of two and a quarter years to cultural studies, a year more to general business sub- jects (which are after all adaptations of academic work), and perhaps three-quarters of a year to secretarial tech- niques. As a result of this type of program, Mary is ready without further education to undertake the work of a secretary. Under present conditions the College has little difficulty in placing her either in some business establishment or as a secretary to a professional man.

Probably the most important thing that any college does for its students is to influence the quality of their thinking and their general attitudes. Aside from this, if Mary Jones chooses to make a career of business, what we have done to develop her business intelligence is far more significant than any skills we have given her, for she possesses a foundation to which she can relate her subsequent experiences. As long as skill in shorthand and typewriting are essential to gaining the first position in business, we shall have to teach them, but we shall hope in time to find new avenues of approach to the more responsible business positions.

You may well ask what the permanent value of all this technical preparation is if Mary Jones marries and leaves business a few years after graduating from college. Granted that the skill-training has served its purpose in enabling her to secure her first position and to be successful in it, what of the time and energy devoted to the fundamental business studies? I need hardly remind you that Mrs. Mary Jones Smith will always be a consumer, and that she will find many occasions in the management of her home and in the activities of her social and personal life to use whatever economic understanding she has gained from the general study of business. It is not claiming too much to say that the appreciative value to be derived from such study will compare favorably with that gained in many courses which make no effort to be useful either vocationally or otherwise.

In my opening remarks, I stated that in the first hundred years of higher education for women, a good deal of effort was devoted to showing that women were capable of pursuing successfully a program of education planned for men. That point may now be taken as proved. Women who look forward to entering the learned professions will perhaps always need that type of education, and some others will always prefer it.

Without being so rash as to prophesy, I would venture to hope that the next few decades will bring a wider recognition of the need for different types of collegiate education for women, to the end that all the Mary Joneses may be well served.

Education and You Young Women

ONE DAY NOT LONG AGO I OPENED
the morning paper to find among other items of news
an announcement that Radcliffe College was considering
"retooling" courses. The gist of the item was that many
women who have raised their children now find themselves with time on their hands. They are intellectually
able, and possibly would like an "intellectual retooling"
that the college would be glad to provide.

Probably many people who read that item that morning said, "Sounds like a smart idea," and passed on to
other news. But no bombs exploded. There was no
flurry of amazement or disbelief. *Of course* women
should continue their intellectual interests in this day
and generation.

But suppose we had been living about two hundred
and fifty years ago — a short time indeed in the long
history of mankind. In the year 1657 Daniel Defoe
would have amazed us with his pronouncement that
women were educable. In his *An Essay On Projects,*
he had this to say about "An Academy for Women:"

"I have often thought of it as one of the most barbarous
customs in the world, considering us as a civilized and a
Christian country, that we deny the advantages of learning
to women. We reproach the sex every day for their folly
and impertinence, while I am confident, had they the advantages of education equal to us, they would be guilty of

21

less than ourselves. One would wonder, indeed, how it should happen that women are conversible at all, since they are only beholden to natural parts for all their knowledge. Their youth is spent to teach them to stitch and sew or make baubles. They are taught to read, indeed, and perhaps to write their names or so, and that is the height of a woman's education. And I would but ask any who slight the sex for their understanding, What is a man . . . good for that is taught no more?"

Having declared his faith in women, he goes on to describe the kind of school they should have.

"The house I would have built in a form by itself, as well as in a place by itself. The building should be of three plain fronts, without any juttings or bearing-work, that the eye might at a glance see from one coin to the other; the gardens walled in the same triangular figure, with a large moat and but one entrance.

"When thus every part of the situation was contrived as well as might be for discovery, and to render intriguing dangerous, I would have no guards, no eyes, no spies set over the ladies, but shall expect them to be tried by the principles of honor and strict virtue. . . .

"Upon this ground I am persuaded such measures might be taken that the ladies might have all the freedom in the world within their own walls, and yet no intriguing, no indecencies, nor scandalous affairs happen. . . .

"In this house the persons who enter should be taught all sorts of breeding suitable to both their genius and their quality, and, in particular, music and dancing, which it would be cruelty to bar the sex of, because they are their darlings; but, besides this, they should be taught language, as particularly French and Italian; and I would venture the injury of giving a woman more tongues than one. They should, as a particular study, be taught all the graces of speech and all the necessary air of conversation, which our common education is so defective in that I need not expose it. They should be brought to read books, and especially history, and so to read as to make them understand the world and be able to know and judge of things when they hear of them. To such whose genius would lead them to it I would deny no sort of learning: but the chief thing in general is to cultivate the understandings of the sex, that they may be capable of all sorts of conversation; that, their parts and judgments being improved, they may be as profitable in their conversation as they are pleasant. . . .

". . . The great distinguishing difference which is seen in the world between men and women is in their education, and this is manifested by comparing it with the difference between one man or woman and another. And herein it is that I take upon me to make such a bold assertion that all the world are mistaken in their practice about women; for I cannot think that God Almighty ever made them so delicate, so glorious creatures, and furnished them with such charms, so agreeable and so delightful to mankind, with souls capable of the same accomplishments with men, and all to be only the stewards of our houses, cooks, and slaves. . . .

"I need not enlarge on the loss the defect of education is to the sex, nor argue the benefit of the contrary practice; it is a thing will be more easily granted than remedied. This chapter is but an essay at the thing; and I refer the practice to those happy days, if ever they shall be, when men shall be wise enough to mend it."

In the course of the next hundred years some progress must have been made in "bringing women to read books" and in "denying them no sort of learning." At least Jane Austen seems to think so. Writing in *Pride and Prejudice* in 1797, she talks of Charlotte Lucas, aged twenty-seven, who has just announced to her family her engagement to Mr. Collins:

"The whole family . . . were properly overjoyed on the occasion. The younger girls formed hopes of *coming out* a year or so sooner than they might otherwise have come; and the boys were relieved from their apprehension of Charlotte's dying an old maid. Charlotte herself was tolerably composed. She had gained her point, and had time

23

to consider of it. Her reflections were in general satisfactory. Mr. Collins, to be sure, was neither amiable nor agreeable; his society was irksome, and his attachment to her must be imaginary. But still he would be her husband. Without thinking highly either of men or of matrimony, marriage had always been her object; it was the only honorable provision for well educated young women of small fortune, and however uncertain of giving happiness, must be their pleasantest preservative from want. This preservative she had now obtained; and at the age of twenty-seven, without having ever been handsome, she felt all the good luck of it."

Jane Austen, who mirrored her time with complete faithfulness, takes for granted that a young woman may be well-educated, but she is not surprised or belligerent about the plight in which this educated young woman finds herself.

What has happened to the education of women from the time of Defoe to the present? You have probably heard of the female seminaries and the finishing schools of the early and middle nineteenth century. Some of these were good schools for their times, but many of them taught little but polite accomplishments to young women of good fortune and family.

You know also that women then set out to prove that what men could learn they too could learn — and that they proved their point. You know that today any woman, far from having to commit herself to a prison-like academy to learn "the graces of speech," may choose whatever kind of learning she wishes.

And what has happened since the days of Jane Austen to the life of the educated young woman? People of my generation have seen opportunities of all kinds, from the simplest job to the most learned profession, open up to her — reluctantly, it is true, and yet completely. Yet today, far from feeling grateful at having accepted an irksome husband, she may elect her own occupation and her own manner of living.

Have we, then, reached goals with which we may feel satisfied? May we go on as we are, forgetting the business of the education of women and the uses to which it is put? The answer on all sides is "No." I say "on all sides" advisedly, for this is literally so. The answer comes from professionals in education, from college women, and from the general public.

I should like to mention two books that challenge much of our current practice: one, *On the Education of Women* by George D. Stoddard, President of the University of Illinois, and the other, *Educating Our Daughters* by Lynn White, Jr., President of Mills College. As you may know, the American Association of University Women has recently conducted an elaborate inquiry among women graduates to learn their views on how our education may be bettered, and *Fortune* magazine has published a survey of public opinion on the values and goals of higher education for men and women separately.

I shall not try to summarize here the arguments *pro* and *con* offered in these and other published discussions. It is enough for me to mention the major questions raised. Should women's education continue to follow the pattern of men's education, or should it be different because women play a different part in life from men? Should occupational training be included in the undergraduate education of women? What should our attitude be on preparing women for their roles as wives and mothers? And implicit throughout is the question: How can we meet new demands and at the same time preserve the fine traditions of our culture?

25

Besides these public questionings, there are the constant discussions that go on among us who, for lack of any more specific occupations or abilities, fall into the category of "educators." We talk endlessly about what education *is* doing and what it *should* do instead. These discussions are likely to divide us into those who think of education primarily in terms of subject matter and those who think first in terms of the needs of the people to be educated. In any group holding diverse views on this subject, some will ally themselves with the functionalists — those who are concerned with the whole person and not solely with the intellect, — and will find themselves opposed by those of the liberal arts tradition, because of an alleged lack of sympathy for scholarship and knowledge for its own sake. And yet, if the discussion continued long enough, spirited though it would be, the opponents would show, I am sure, wide areas of agreement and some of compromise, with the areas of no compromise surprisingly small — smaller even than they would have been a few years ago.

My conclusion, then, is that we have not yet obtained One World in the education of women. This is by no means a drawback. We shall always need to revise our purposes, to experiment with new ideas, and to seek unifying principles. This being so, women's education, subject of so much debate and attack, will need the help of all men and women, whether educators or not, and especially the best thinking and strongest support of those women who have received the benefits of a college education.

This foreshortened review of women's education has the serious purpose of pointing out how favored the experience of such women has been. But herein lies a certain danger, that *those who have had great advantages may become too specialized or even exclusive in their interests. For the safety of democracy, that must not be.*

It is easy to oversimplify cause and effect. At the risk of doing so, I will state my conviction that it would be impossible for a democracy to thrive without educating *all* its people. The Founding Fathers proclaimed this — not with their first breath, but with their second. After something like order began to emerge from their efforts to found a nation, many of them — Washington, Jefferson, Madison, John Jay, and others — wrote of the need to educate the people, who were the final source of power.

Today the people are still the final source of power in a democracy grown huge and complicated. Their education is still of the utmost importance to the general welfare, and all of us, whatever our circumstances, our experience, or our interests, should give our attention to the *public* schools. It is here that nearly all the citizens of our Democracy are being trained. How are they being trained? What are they learning, and in what way? Are the schools laboratories in the practice of democratic principles, both for the children and for the community? Many other questions come to mind, and I shall not try to answer or even ask them all. My purpose is merely to give an awareness of the problem, in the hope that we may all make it our personal concern.

In Colonial times we continued our "learning" in the only way we knew — that brought from the old world. On the whole, this learning was for the privileged. The idea of educating everyone began to appear in the writings of the Founding Fathers when they were free to contemplate what they had wrought. They had brought into being a leviathan — universal suffrage for men — and they saw that it needed to be made safe. Jefferson, writing in 1816, said:

27

"If a nation expects to be ignorant and free in a state of civilization it expects what never was and never will be. . . . There is no safe deposit [for the functions of government] but with the people themselves: nor can they be safe with them without information."

James Madison echoed this conviction when he wrote:

"A popular government without popular information or the means of acquiring it is but a prologue to a farce or a tragedy or, perhaps, both. Knowledge will forever govern ignorance; and a people who seem to be their own governors must arm themselves with the power which knowledge gives."

In this as in other ideas the Founding Fathers were farsighted. Under our constitution, the control of education rested with the states, and the states moved in their own time. Gradually, common schools came into being, but it was not until 1852 that any state made attendance compulsory. In that year Massachusetts passed a law requiring everyone between the ages of eight and fourteen to attend school at least twelve weeks a year. A hundred years later we find that all the children in the nation must attend school most of the year, usually until they are sixteen, but in some states, eighteen. Meanwhile our population has increased six-fold and has become so heterogeneous that it was our pride a generation ago to call ourselves "The Melting Pot." This vast and varied mass of young people must now stay in school nearly up to the time of their adulthood. The climate in which their learning must take place is that of a post-war world in which the spirit of war is a normal state, with democracy challenged and our nation forced into the role of a leading world power. So what happens to the minds of our great school population and what their experiences in our Democracy are — these are matters of first importance. Do you wonder that I say, "Whatever our other interests, we must give our attention to the public schools?"

Strangely enough, in the field of education it has often proved easier for us to understand the ends and discuss the means to those ends, than to know what we might do to be of help. What specifically *can* we do for the public schools? One thing we can do is to see that the right people are elected to our local school committees. Who are these right people? They are those who will select and support able and honest school officials. They will employ the best qualified teachers wherever they may be found, and then respect their professional knowledge of what should be taught and how taught. The right school-committeemen will work to provide the tools which the teachers need, and to pay them salaries commensurate with the importance of their work. They can be counted on to support the principle of freedom in teaching and to defend the teacher's civil rights. Their interest in being on the school committee will not stem from a desire for political advancement or for special privileges for themselves and others. In short, their sole concern will be to render a disinterested service to the youth of the community.

Another thing we can do is to help create public opinion in support of good schools. Unfortunately not all college graduates in a community can be counted on to take a balanced view of what our public schools should do. Sometimes there is apathy — especially among those sending their own children to private and parochial schools — or outright hostility toward any improvement that will increase the tax-rate. At other times, such people express a narrow concern for the education of the prospective college-goers without recognizing that the public schools must serve *all* the children of *all* the people. Even in 1954 it is only a minority of high school graduates who go on to higher institutions, and though we must serve this group well, we must be equally concerned that the young people who do not go to college are also well served. A good school committee needs a strong public opinion back of it. As intelligent citizens aware of the importance of good public schools, the college-bred can help others to see their significance, and so strengthen their support in the community.

They might also work for better schools by taking part in special projects of the Parent-Teacher Association, the League of Women Voters, or other community groups. Such activities in and of themselves may seem small and inconsequential. They are not. Taken together they add up to a significant whole.

Though in our nation the public schools are a function of the state, the state wisely leaves much to the local community. By identifying ourselves with efforts to improve public schools in our own community we will be doing our part to ensure the health of Democracy.

The College of Tomorrow

In the spring of 1939 I attended a meeting in Boston at which an authority on international affairs discussed the growing tensions in Europe. He raised the question whether the complex of forces there would lead to war. His uncompromising answer was "No;" and he went on for fifteen or twenty minutes explaining why there would be no war in Europe. Six months later, war broke out. The moral is that if we must prophesy it is safe to do so only with respect to the far-distant future when we will be dead or at least when our hearers will have forgotten what we said.

So this talk, the title of which seems to demand a prediction of the changes that will take place in the American college or a perhaps somewhat fanciful description of the ideal college in the ideal society, will attempt neither. I intend to discuss some of the changes that are already in process, and leave it to you and the future to judge which of these changes are likely to have a permanent effect on higher education.

There is a truism that in any country at any time, education is dictated by the dominant social ideals. A moment's reflection suggests that even though we may not know a great deal about the schools and colleges of other lands, we are familiar with the class structure of education in England which reflects the class structure of England itself; with the propaganda schools of Soviet Russia which reflect the dictatorship of that country; and with the modification of the German school system with the advent of the Republic and its subsequent modification with the coming of the dictatorship. Little proof is needed to demonstrate the truth that at any time in any country, the schools and colleges reflect the currents of thought, the social ideals and attitudes of the people. And so it is no wonder that in this country during the past ten or twenty years, rather profound changes have occurred in our educational thinking, changes that have paralleled the changes in our social and economic and political thought.

On every hand today we see colleges of standing seeking new answers to the three fundamental questions of higher education: Whom shall we teach? What shall we teach? and How shall we teach? Any attempt to answer these questions exhaustively in a brief essay is of course impossible; and I shall try to answer the first with some care; the second more cursorily; and leave the answer to the third to be implied in those of the others.

I

Those of us who have attended college and are familiar with college experience and practice know that the standard procedure, traditional in American colleges, is to require certain definite background studies in the secondary schools as conditions of entrance. Colleges vary greatly in their detailed requirements, but the usual pattern is, so much English, so much foreign language, so much history, so much science; and these may in some instances be certified by the secondary school and in others tested by examinations. But the significant fact is that it is a common practice of American colleges, and has been for many years, to define a certain type of previous education as a condition to acceptance by the institution.

There has been a growing dissatisfaction with this practice, and numerous investigations have called into question its validity. I should like to cite one or two instances of the kind of thinking now directed upon the important problem of whom we shall teach in college.

I take my first illustration from a study made at Ohio State University, a public institution — and public institutions tend to admit a larger range of students than do independent or privately endowed colleges: that is, they are less selective in their admission requirements. And yet this study could be duplicated, I believe, in most colleges.

Ohio State University examined its incoming freshmen in certain fundamental abilities which, most of us will agree, are essential to successful intellectual work: ability to read, to read rapidly, to read understandingly; ability to write the English language effectively and clearly; ability to deal with quantitive processes drawn mostly from mathematics.

Some interesting facts emerged. First of all it was found that 30 per cent of the freshman class could not read with any greater rapidity than the average eighth-grade child in the public schools. In a college more selective the percentage would undoubtedly be lower; but I believe that there are substantial numbers of pupils, coming with presumably excellent high-school records, who, judged by objective examinations, cannot read as well as the average eighth-grade pupil. In speed and comprehension of reading, 7 per cent could not understand material of average difficulty for an eighth-grade group. In writing the English language, 11 per cent were inferior to ninth-grade standards. In arithmetic, 50 per cent were below seventh-grade standards in long division, and in other operations varied from that down to 4 per cent, inferior to seventh-grade norms. This is one type of evidence that tends to suggest how traditional methods of selection do not produce a homogeneous group of students, capable of going on from a point conceived by the college as a necessary preliminary to college work.

You may have seen in the newspapers the results of a study by the Carnegie Foundation, published in 1938, of the growth of students in Pennsylvania through high school and college. For the purpose the Foundation used a comprehensive knowledge test, built on academic subject matter, such as is commonly required in the college-preparatory programs and also forms a large part of the college program. It was found that 25 per cent of college sophomores were not as well informed on this material as the average high school senior, and that about 25 per cent of the seniors about to graduate from college were not as well informed as the average sophomore. The findings further showed that there were high-school seniors already better informed in this test than some of the college seniors, four years older, and 25 per cent of the college sophomores were superior to the average college senior.

Is any further evidence needed of the failure of our present methods of selection to find for the college a supply of students homogeneous either as regards the abilities they bring with them or their progress after admission?

Another type of study bearing on the same point, that traditional methods of selection are not adequate, concerns how important it is that students shall have had a secondary education dominantly concerned with languages and mathematics; because most college preparatory programs are of that sort. There have been a number of investigations of the validity of this emphasis. I shall cite two briefly.

One was an investigation conducted jointly more than ten years ago by the Universities of Kentucky, Indiana, and Cincinnati. The conclusion of this careful study was that there was no relationship between the subjects studied in high school and subsequent college success. The pattern was unimportant. Students who took a good deal of vocational work in high school, and they were many, tended to shift to academic subjects in college, and were successful despite their lack of academic studies in high school; and the opposite was also true. The study concludes with the statement: "What a student has studied prior to coming to college seems to have no bearing upon his subsequent success; the important thing is how well he did whatever he undertook on the secondary level." Such a conclusion raises serious questions with respect to traditional admission requirements, based on a certain pattern of work.

A more recent investigation — the eight-year study conducted by the Progressive Education Association — confirms this evidence. At a recent meeting of the Association of American Colleges in Philadelphia, Dean Hawkes of Columbia, an active member of the Commission on School and College Relations of the Progressive Education Association, made a report on how well graduates of thirty progressive schools were doing in college. It should be explained that a great many colleges agreed, some six or seven years ago, to accept students from these thirty schools, regardless of the colleges' published admission requirements, and to evaluate the records of these students entirely in terms of whatever preparation the progressive schools had de-

35

cided to offer. It is therefore interesting to study the college success of these students; and it was on that point that Dean Hawkes was reporting. He said, in the March 20, 1940, *Association of American Colleges Bulletin:*

"The results of this study seem to indicate that the pattern of preparatory school program which concentrates on a preparation for a fixed set of entrance examinations is not the only satisfactory means of fitting a boy or girl for making the most out of the college experience. It looks as if the capacities and interests of the students are fully as important as the pattern of subject matter studied, and apparently the stimulus and initiative which the less conventional approach to secondary education affords sends on to college students as well, if not better, prepared for the college experience than comparable students who have had the more traditional preparation."

Other studies — one made by the University of Oregon, for example — confirm these conclusions. One may properly raise the question why we persist in our present kind of admission requirement.

Before I leave this subject, I must point out that there is another finding in the Carnegie Report that seems extremely important for any group concerned with deciding whom we shall admit to college. The Pennsylvania study reveals the fact that out of a thousand high school youngsters only 175 go to college, and of the 175, 105 are successful. Sixty-seven failed in the college experience. Taking the 105 of the total 1,000, do they represent all or nearly all of the students who have the ability to do college work? The Carnegie Foundation, in examining the records of those who did not go to college, found that for every 105 successful in college, 174 others were equally capable, but did not go to college. These facts suggest that somewhere in our society, with all our efforts to extend educational opportunity and approach something like an equalization of it, we are still far from offering it to all those capable of profiting from it. For every student now in college, there are one and a half who might be, judging by their ability, but who are not. There is very obviously a substantial reservoir of pupils who could profit by college experience, without any modification of existing standards of what constitutes college work.

If we go further and consider the young persons between the ages of eighteen and twenty-two who do not quite qualify by existing standards, we may ask whether they are not also educable to some degree. Could not the colleges conceivably devise some program of study that would be worth while for them, even if not what we conceive to be a college education? There are already signs that youth will not be denied further advanced educational opportunities, whether the colleges intend to be selective, or to encourage students not now considered eligible to attend, or to extend their program downward. At any rate, we can be very sure that the growing body of information will lead to a more intelligent appraisal of which students shall attend.

II

To pass now to my second question, the more important and really the meat of this discussion: What shall we teach in college?

Much has been said and written on it in these troublous times, with widespread criticism of what colleges are not teaching. I think, however, that there is a measure of agreement between opposing philosophies; agreement at least on the facts of the situation. Critics of college education in America agree that the curriculum has ceased to be the center of the student's interest; extra-curricular activities loom large in his mind; athletics are tremendously overemphasized; and fraternities, sororities, and social life occupy a disproportionate amount of his interest. They also maintain that, because the curriculum does not attract them, students in large numbers are not going to college. Such critics will readily agree that a large number of serious-minded students are in college and that in some colleges their numbers form a large proportion. But they still point out that students in general seem to find their main interest anywhere, everywhere, except in their studies. They will also agree that the elective system, introduced by President Eliot of Harvard and quickly spreading all over the country, however valuable it may be in giving flexibility to what was formerly a very rigid program, has been carried to a point where it now permits an excessive amount of specialization and has to some extent produced a disintegration of the curriculum.

It can hardly be denied that in most colleges courses are offered because teachers want to offer them, rather than because students want to take them. Having space in their program to offer a new course, they urge the offering of one they wish to give, perhaps because they have a special group of students in mind or, more frequently, because it permits them a wider range of self-expression. Whatever the reason, it must be obvious to any student of college curricula today that we are offering a confusing variety of courses, and that main courses tend to split up into smaller and smaller ones, each covering a relatively restricted field of subject matter. Critics of college education argue that the elective system has permitted some students to specialize in one area practically to the exclusion of all else, and has led to a disintegration of the general curriculum by permitting students to add and add courses, without any effort to integrate their programs round any concept of general knowledge or of a well-informed mind. The result is that many college graduates fail to show in life much evidence of having profited by college. They have closed minds. Many rarely read good books; many promptly put their brains in the waste-basket, so to speak, upon receiving the degree. Their lives do not distinguish them from others who have not been to college. This is not true of all, by any means, but is still true of a great many.

If you had attended, as I have, meetings of the Association of American Colleges, and had heard college presidents talk about what their major problems are, you would have found that they are mainly three: fights with alumni or alumnae; conflicts about athletics; and disputes between the ROTC and the Peace Society or other organizations of opposing opinion. These are, however, college problems rather than curriculum problems, though all, especially the first, may affect the educational attitudes of students. If the alumni of the American college cannot be trusted to take an intelligent and enlightened attitude toward progressive modifications of the curriculum, toward curbing the defects which informed critics see in colleges, does not this fact reflect in some degree on the success of the colleges themselves in developing appropriate attitudes and ways of thinking in their students about new problems in new times?

What higher education needs, and is trying to find, is one underlying principle to correct the disintegration of the curriculum just described. Opinion on what this underlying principle is takes two quite different points of view; and at the risk of oversimplification I should like to discuss these in terms of two definitely antagonistic conceptions competing for influence in higher education today. I shall call one the Hutchins point of view and the other the Dewey point of view.

The names are familiar to everybody: Robert M. Hutchins, President of the University of Chicago; and John Dewey, former professor of philosophy at Columbia University and before that at the University of Chicago. John Dewey, perhaps more than any other person, has contributed to the philosophy of education in this country and has influenced the evolution of schooling at all levels. I am not a Hutchins man or a Dewey man, and shall probably do violence to the views of both. I am glad neither is present to challenge my interpretation; but if they do not mean what I shall say, then I don't think they write very clearly. They perhaps should have a course in English composition.

I gather that Mr. Hutchins contends that liberal education in this country has failed because it does not make men free; and it has failed to make men free because it has avoided self-discipline, intellectual discipline. The result has been what he calls decay of the creative powers of the mind, especially in speculative thought. He believes further that the drift of modern education away from the historic content has permitted talents and energies of youth to be dissipated in unwholesome substitutes for the intellectual life. He would propose, therefore, a return to the intellectual life, to discipline, to the development of human talents through direct intellectual materials.

In a little book entitled *The Higher Learning in America,* he outlines a program for general education. It is stated in Chapter III, and has been since set forth in a series of articles in the *Saturday Evening Post.* I will summarize his views of education on the junior-college level.

He advocates for general education a course of study of the greatest books of the western world, and of the arts of reading, writing, thinking, and speaking, together with mathematics, the best example of the process of human reasoning. If our hope has been to frame a curriculum reducing to its elements our common human nature, this program should realize that object. If we wish to prepare the young for intelligent action, this course of study should assist us. The young will have learned what has been done in the past, and what the greatest men have thought. They will have learned to think for themselves. Students and professors will acquire a common stock of ideas and common methods of dealing with them. All the needs of general education in America seem to be satisfied by this curriculum.

He goes on to discuss whether it will work and what the objections to it are, especially the objection that students won't like it very well, that they will find it too hard; but he maintains that they can acquire the necessary discipline to pursue the program of perfection he has in mind. He concludes his comments on the objections as follows:

"No, the students can do the work if the faculties will let them. Will the faculties let them? I doubt it. The professors of today have been brought up differently. Not all of them have read all the books they would have to teach. Not all of them are ready to change the habits of their lives. In the meanwhile, they will bring up their successors so that the next group will have the habits they have had themselves, and the love of money, a misconception of democracy, a false notion of progress, and a distorted idea of utility, and the antagonism to which all these lead, conspire to confirm their conviction that it is more discipline which is needed. The times call for the establishment of a new college or for an evangelistic movement which shall have for its object the conversion of the individual, and of the teaching profession, to a true conception of general education. Unless some such demonstration can take place, we shall remain in our confusion. We shall have neither general education nor universities and we shall continue to disappoint the hope of our people."

Now I think that is a fair sample of Mr. Hutchins's point of view as to what needs to be done to college education. Before I examine it I should like to give the opposing view, that of what I call the Dewey camp. I do not know that John Dewey has written anything directly bearing on our subject of the college of tomorrow; but many people have adopted his general philosophy of education and adapted it, with whatever modifications, to the college curriculum. His philosophy is that the curriculum should be built around present-day personal and social needs of youth. The student should learn to solve problems, not by going off in a corner and learning to think, but by solving them here and now. This is not a training for tomorrow, but for interpreting the problems of today. Again and again the Dewey philosophy suggests that there is no better preparation for tomorrow than in an education that teaches the individual to meet the needs and exigencies of the present.

To be fair I will read a passage, not from Dewey, but from President Constance Warren of Sarah Lawrence College, a so-called progressive college, founded to set forth the Dewey philosophy. Miss Warren is discussing *A New Design in Education:*

"Each student, we believe, has within herself the seeds of what she is capable of becoming. The purpose of her college education is to enable her to develop these innate qualities and grow into a mature individual, emotionally and intellectually capable of coming to terms with whatever life may have in store for her. How is this desire to be achieved? It is no simple cut-and dried matter. There is no perfect curriculum; no average student; no royal road to learning. We must ask ourselves how to find what the individual needs to help her to understand herself, realize her own powers, and develop a sense of direction and purpose. We must open her eyes to the world about her and awaken in her a sense of obligation to society. What can be done to make the whole process of education more fruitful must be broken down into a score of searching questions." Miss Warren then goes on to raise a whole paragraph of questions, brought to mind by this general philosophy. She next says:

"What is the essence of [this] new approach to education? It is individualized education, adapted to the different capacities, interests and objectives of individual students, to the best of the faculty's ability to understand, recognize, and satisfy such differing needs. The curriculum must be flexible to serve individual ends, and cannot be considered as an end in itself, or a strait jacket to fit all alike. We are convinced that the student's desire to learn is fully as important as her innate ability. One with ordinary ability and strong motivations will often accomplish more than another with superior talent who lacks that vital spark. Incentives developed from within make for effective self-discipline, where constant use of force or authority from without breeds dependence, or resistance, and postpones maturity."

Here we have the extremes in our educational thinking, both working toward modification of the college. They agree in being dissatisfied with colleges as they are, because they do not foster in any large numbers of students the self-discipline leading to a developed power to be used after college days are over; but they are at the poles as to the way to attain that end. I don't believe John Dewey would disagree with Robert Hutchins as to what he wants to accomplish, but I know he would disagree violently as to method. And we have already seen that Hutchins has little sympathy for the Dewey approach.

43

One may characterize the two views in this way. Hutchins is interested in a body of abstract ideas which are imposed upon the student from without. He hopes the student will like them. He believes the student can be led to like them, but he is primarily concerned with the ideas and methods of thought the student will use in a variety of settings. Dewey, on the other hand, is interested in what goes on in the individual. He is not interested in imposing ideas from the outside. He wants to look inside the student and develop his traits in contact with materials, hoping that in the long run the student will read answer to answer and become interested in ideas, processes of thought, by recognizing them as essential to the solution of his own personal and social problems. Hutchins would say we can define a common body of truth which lies at the base of all education. We find it in the ideas that have lived through the ages. Dewey would say that the content appropriate for education cannot be defined until we know the character of the individual student, and his needs. Hutchins insists on extreme intellectualism; Dewey, on utilitarianism in the broadest sense.

"Utilitarianism" is one of the words that stimulate opposition. Like "red" or "communism" it carries an emotional content. I wish I had half an hour to discuss it and its true meaning in education, for I think its meaning can be extended to include anything worth learning, even the most abstract. As I understand Dewey, he is interested in utilitarianism in its broadest sense. Let's not give the dog a bad name and hang it. As for Hutchins, he tends to ignore what psychologists have discovered about the psychology of learning, while Dewey uses it.

But I do not wish to imply that there is no possibility of success in the Hutchins approach. Though I must be somewhat abstract, I should say a word further about it. All we know about training people to reason logically can be summed up in some such way as this: The best way to learn to think logically is to practice on material as like as possible to that on which we will want to think logically in practical experience. There is, in other words, no best material; though Hutchins thinks there is, and finds it in mathematics. I suggest however that no one has ever measured the growth of logical power or reasoning that mathematics produces in Hutchins' program or proved that such a power developed in one situation is of use in all kinds of situations. I suspect from the evidence that the Hutchins experiment will not prove that there is any one best material for developing reasoning power; but honesty compels me to say that nobody knows that the experiment will fail, even though the subject has been studied very extensively.

I must be more specific and show what, in terms of college programs, the two points of view lead to. We have heard much of the experiment now in progress at St. John's College in Maryland, where Mr. Hutchins is president of the Board of Trustees and two men who are closely associated with him in the University of Chicago are respectively President and Dean of the college: Mr. Stringfellow Barr and Mr. Scott Buchanan. They have taken the old college and remodeled it according to the formula for general education outlined by Mr. Hutchins in *The Higher Learning in America.*

The curriculum is prescribed alike for all students, no allowance being made for individual election. The core of the curriculum is the hundred great books written in the past, and these must be read by the students during their four-year course. The first year's study ends with the Alexandrian Age; the second, with the

Middle Ages; the third, with the middle of the 18th Century; and the fourth, with the present. There are other phases of the program I cannot go into. If you are interested in the list of great books, it is given in Adler's *How to Read a Book*.

At St. John's students seem to read twenty-five books a year, or about a book every ten days. One wonders whether freshmen can get the training in logic Mr. Hutchins speaks of by spending ten days on Plato's *Republic* — about all of Plato they will have time for. Even though reading a hundred books in four years may not seem too much, when we take into account the number of subjects they raise needing careful study, we can only wonder whether the books can be handled in any but a superficial manner. Intensive courses in Shakespeare may devote themselves for a whole month to one play, and only some elements in that play. How much training in logical reasoning can result from reading Plato in ten days?

The other institution I wish to discuss is the University of Chicago, where the experiment is not so extreme as at St. John's, but has much the same point of view. The undergraduate in the lower division — that is, the first two years of the program — studies physical sciences, biological sciences, social sciences, humanities, English composition, and ethics. He takes comprehensive examinations whenever he feels prepared to do so. He is eligible for advanced study in the upper division when he has passed. Time does not permit my going into detail. I will leave the subject of intellectualism by raising what would seem appropriate doubts about its solving the problems that affect the personal and social needs of the students.

For comparison let us turn to another experimental college, Stephens Junior College at Columbia, Missouri, because it has made a new approach based on the philosophy of Dewey: that the curriculum should be based on the actual activities of people in life and society. What kinds of activities are the students going to enter in the future? From an analysis of this question conclusions are drawn about a proper curriculum. The subjects of study do not sound like those of any other college: communications, social adjustment, physical health, consumers' problems, philosophy of living, appreciation of the beautiful. At Minnesota General College, where similar ideas are followed, the curriculum is divided into four parts: personal life orientation, social and civic orientation, general vocational orientation, and home and family-life orientation. These four cover our entire lives: personal life, communal life, working life, and family life. The curriculum falls nicely into these four categories.

Less extreme illustrations of the same tendency in education are found in more conservative colleges, attempting to modify their curricula in the direction of meeting the personal and social needs of students. I need only to cite the numerous survey courses developed at Columbia and elsewhere that cut across fields like history, government, economics, and sociology; and the four-year program at Hobart College, where every student every college year has at least one course in education for citizenship; and the winter period at Bennington College, where the students have the advantage of working for an extended time on a project related to their major interest, and are free to travel to urban centers to take positions in stores or settlement houses and study their problems in the actual community setting.

All of these are efforts to bring the community and the curriculum closer together. In fact most colleges straddle the two today. The Hutchins idea is more conservative: it is, in fact, the point of view of scholarship. The other plans seek to adapt the curriculum to individual needs. Assuming that the latter idea remains in the ascendancy, as I believe it is today, we should face for a moment the question of vocational needs.

Am I going to get a job? is the question uppermost in the mind of youth at present. That this is so is indicated by the study made by the American Council on Education in Maryland, for the American Youth Commission, a study seeking the opinions of youth between the ages of sixteen and twenty-four. Thirteen hundred answered the questionnaires, and a very large proportion said that the job was their major problem. I quote: "If a hundred of these youths were each asked to state what in his or her opinion was the crux of the problem, our data would further indicate that sixty-five would characterize it as basically economic." To me this means jobs, many jobs; to some it would mean wages sufficient to permit a higher standard of living; to others, a deeper sense of security and a more hopeful promise of vocational adjustment; and to still others, an income making marriage or further education possible. The job is of maximum importance to youth. It is therefore important to the college of tomorrow.

There are a good many colleges without vocational studies in which the vocational figures largely, nevertheless. At Berea College vocational experience is used as a means of livelihood for students while attending; at Antioch, students spend part of their time in study and part on the job. But in neither of these is the vocational regarded as integral in the educational program. It is supplementary. In fact training-work has been accepted as a part of college education for a good many years. But Eastern colleges interested in progressive

48

developments are reluctant to admit the vocational on even terms with other objectives.

Professor Russell of the University of Chicago has made a study of thirty-five colleges that showed distinctive features in their curricula. Only two or three, among them Simmons, insisted on professional preparation as an essential part of general education. A few others mentioned vocational orientation; but most of the colleges were careful to point out that the vocational had no part in their conception of general education. We have a long way to go before we can expect any general recognition of what seems to me fairly obvious, that if the personal and social needs of the student are central, we cannot set vocational problems apart from those of home and family life and social and civic responsibility. If these are general education, can the vocational be something different? It seems to me the college of tomorrow will have to face that question; and I believe that in the long run it will come to accept the vocational as a part of general education.

I have not said much about how we shall teach, but think that what I have said suggests an answer. Helping and guiding the student to be self-directing in his learning is the purpose of all plans for improvement in college education. If you read the book I have mentioned, by Constance Warren, you will learn that the students of Sarah Lawrence College get very little class instruction. They take only three courses a year, each meeting for one two-hour period a week — six hours' instruction. In addition they have one hour of individual conference with their teachers, a total of nine hours of experience in contact with the faculty. The tendency shown here, of shifting learning to the students as rapidly as possible, is becoming general elsewhere.

Miss Warren has a very interesting discussion of the failures as well as the successes of the system in accomplishing that end. The purpose is to guide the student to be self-directing in his learning and in his efforts to secure mastery of a special field.

The Swarthmore honor plan selects the ablest students at the end of the sophomore year and sets them entirely free from class exactions, an experience covering a wide range of interests — that is, a wide range within a broad subject — and outside examiners are engaged to determine success or failure. The tutorial system and general examinations at Harvard are manifestations of the same tendency. Emphasizing self-dependence in learning lets the faculty from under as soon as possible. Many colleges recognize the value of an informal relationship between teachers and taught: Bennington, Bard, Black Mountain, Sarah Lawrence — notably progressive colleges again. Still other colleges are raising serious question respecting the traditional concept of the relationship between research and teaching, in the undergraduate teacher's job. I should like to say something on that subject.

The traditional idea is that to be a good college teacher one must be a productive scholar as well; otherwise one will dry up, cease to grow, have nothing new to offer. To me that statement is no more true than if we turned it around and said that a scholar must be a productive teacher or he ceases to be a scholar. I think it is obviously false. There are many men and women engaged in productive scholarship who have never done any teaching but are successful as scholars. We need in our colleges a conception of scholarship which is not limited to what is known as productive research. I can only believe that teachers in an institution like Sarah Lawrence College are continuing to grow although they do not engage in research. But their scholarship comes through the study of the problems of the individual student and of the wealth of knowledge that must be brought to bear on that student's education. I do not see how one can go stale with such a point of view.

I think the sounder conception is that there is a scholarship in the teaching process itself, and that emphasis on the traditional type of scholarship may lead a person away from interest in teaching and in its improvement, rather than towards it. Many of the difficulties we now face in college education are attributable to lack of interest by the administration in the improvement of teaching. Administrations recognize improvement of the faculty in research. Both the professor and the college acquire a reputation by publishing books. The "productive" man is in demand. Other colleges want him. But the teacher is more likely to have only a local reputation. Teaching is extremely difficult to evaluate. Who are the good teachers? Instead of trying to answer that question, I think administrators tend to ask of a professor what he has contributed to the prestige of the institution. He may be a poor teacher, but he has written books.

But there is a point of view, and a justifiable one, that teaching is an honorable career in itself, even though a teacher may not wish to be a research scholar or his research takes the form of acquainting himself with the subject of teaching and its adaptation to the education of youth. Colleges in search of vital teachers are finding it difficult to discover men and women who have the capacity for developing young people as learners, as self-educators. It is time that more attention was given to this.

In summary I shall propose some conclusions, justified, I believe, with respect to the college of tomorrow.

1. Colleges will in future provide opportunities for a much larger number of adolescent youth than at present.

2. Colleges will hereafter be less concerned with what a student has learned already than with his promise for further learning.

3. In their search for a unifying principle in programs, colleges will come to rely more and more on the functional view represented by Dewey than on the developmental view represented by Hutchins.

4. The organization of courses will be less influenced by the demands of scholarship than by the personal and social needs of the student. The result will be a breaking down of the barriers now tending to divide departments.

5. Colleges will become increasingly concerned with the problem of the vocational needs of their students and will eventually accept vocational preparation as a part of general education for those whose formal education will terminate with graduation from college.

6. The responsibility for guiding the student's learning will be shifted progressively from the teacher to the student, to the end that he may become an independent learner for the rest of his days.

To my mind, the award of the college degree will come to mean that the student has grasped the opportunity for self-education provided in a program appropriate to him; that he gives promise of adapting himself in his personal and social relationships to the outside world; and that he possesses the social conscience and the will to make himself a constructive force in the community of which he is a part.

Part two

The College and Vocational Education

THE EXTENT TO WHICH THE American college should undertake vocational preparation is one of the most puzzling questions facing higher education today. On the one hand we find proponents of the idea that the chief functions of the college are to transmit the social heritage of the race, to develop and stimulate cultural interests, and to discipline the mind for intelligent thought and action. Many who adhere to this position view vocational preparation with hostility because of a belief that the vocational represents the antithesis to the cultural. On the other hand there is an increasing number who believe that the colleges must face the fact that earning a livelihood is a major necessity of living, and that higher institutions that ignore the vocational are something less than liberal.

Without entering into a discussion of the relative merits of these opposing views, may I affirm my belief that all colleges should take cognizance of vocational preparation. For those young men and women who have enough money to pay for more than four years of college education, graduation from a liberal arts college, followed by technical work in a professional school, may offer a superior approach to a future occupation. But even for these more privileged students, the college should accept the responsibility in guiding

55

their choice of an occupation and their selection of a professional school.

For the many whose formal education will end with the attainment of a bachelor's degree, the college faces a more complex task. It must lay a foundation of cultural experience and at the same time provide for effective participation in occupational life.

The college which thus acknowledges its responsibility for vocational preparation must define its educational philosophy in the fields it seeks to serve. Shall it adopt the view that the best progress is to be found by developing in its students those techniques that workers in the field must possess? Or shall it rather seek to lay a foundation of vocational intelligence on which the worker can develop his own techniques? If the college adopts the former view, its program of vocational preparation will be one of training rather than of education. Its graduates will be as well prepared to undertake skilled tasks as the graduates of a trade school, but no better, except as their level of general cultivation is higher. The college should recognize that the occupations for which it offers vocational preparation must be those that demand superior intelligence and adaptability; and that the best type of preparation is that which aims at a high level of vocational understanding. It cannot be emphasized too strongly that *training* in skills and techniques must occupy a place subordinate to *education* in basic principles in any defensible program of college vocational preparation.

Professional associations through their knowledge of conditions in the field can do much to assist the college in its efforts to lay the foundations of future professional leadership. Unfortunately the type of program best suited to develop such leadership over the long range cannot always produce workers who are immediately skillful — a fact that needs wider recognition among professional associations. There is danger that the program of vocational preparation in college may be hampered by the attempt of standardizing agencies to prescribe courses, subject-matter, and time-allotments minutely. Although such efforts may be fruitful in protecting the field against the graduates of weaker institutions, they will, if persisted in, circumscribe too narrowly the work of the stronger institutions, and hence prevent the attainment of that professional excellence so earnestly sought.

Standards of professional preparation should therefore be defined in terms of goals to be achieved rather than of procedures to be followed. When thus defined, they constitute a constructive force in that they encourage experimentation and varied lines of approach by institutions that aspire to excellence. In their common interest the college and the professional association should work out together such standards as will secure for the profession workers who are not only technically competent but professionally wise.

The Future of the A.B. Degree

Liberal-Technical Education for Women

AT THE OUTSET, I WANT TO MAKE clear my position on certain ideas.

In the first place, I am not at all interested in distinctions between the A. B., the S. B., or any other general baccalaureate degrees. Such distinctions have become largely meaningless with the growth in diversity of undergraduate programs.

Nor am I interested in any efforts springing from a desire on the part of colleges to protect their vested interests. I will not join in any fight to preserve a particular type of curriculum on the ground that it has an established tradition behind it.

My sole interest, and I hope your sole interest in thinking about the future of the A. B. degree at this time, lies in the fact that the wholesale adjustments colleges are making give us the best opportunity we may have for years to come to plan intelligently for the future of women's education.

I have been asked to set forth the point of view of the group of colleges that combine liberal education with technical and professional preparation. In complying with the request I wish to be understood as believing that such colleges represent one stage in the evolution of women's education toward something more adequate than anything we have at present. I may be pardoned for believing that such colleges represent the highest stage yet reached in that evolution.

I can best state the position taken by the liberal-technical college for women if I reduce it to a series of propositions.

A. General Considerations

1. The fundamental objectives of all education at the college level have to do with the development of intellectual and esthetic abilities, and social attitudes.

2. To be of greatest value these abilities and attitudes must be acquired under circumstances similar to those in which they are subsequently to be called forth.

3. Accordingly, that curriculum is best which recognizes and anticipates the kinds of problems graduates will need to meet.

4. The areas in which these problems will arise may be classified as having to do with (a) home and family life; (b) the life of the community; (c) occupational life; and (d) the personal and inner life of the individual.

5. "Liberal" or "cultural" education has in the past been concerned with all of these areas except occupational life.

6. There is no *versus* between "liberal" and "vocational" education: together they constitute "general" education.

B. Considerations Affecting the Vocational Education of College Women

1. Today, as never before, college women are looking forward to self-support in an occupation which will challenge their abilities.

2. Of those who enter college, a relatively small proportion will undertake professional education in graduate

schools. The majority will complete their formal education upon receiving the bachelor's degree.

3. For those who go on to graduate study, the occupational function of the college takes the form of vocational guidance. For the majority who will not go beyond the bachelor's degree, the occupational function of the college requires both vocational guidance and technical education.

4. Since women students almost without exception have as their ultimate goal marriage, home, and children, a prolonged period of professional preparation (such as many men undertake) is not economically or sociologically justifiable in most instances.

5. The occupations which challenge the abilities of college women are those in which there is a large intellectual content — for example, work in schools, libraries, laboratories, social agencies, health agencies, publishing houses, and business establishments.

6. The range of such occupations open to women graduates without technical preparation has steadily declined. Apprenticeship is no answer to vocational preparation.

7. The ideal program of occupational education for college women is one which recognizes the dual objectives of job and marriage. At one and the same time it must serve well those who must support themselves in the interim between graduation and marriage, and those who are entering upon a career which may or may not be combined with marriage.

8. Such a program must combine technical intelligence and technical skill, the former being essential to the building of a career, the latter necessary to placement and success in the first job.

9. Technical intelligence is the body of ideas and principles basic to an occupational field. Its content,

drawn from the arts and sciences, is fundamentally intellectual in character.

10. Thus viewed, technical education is capable of synthesis with the social, civic, and cultural phases of liberal education to the end that both society and the individual may be well served.

In setting forth the foregoing propositions, I should be remiss if I left you with the idea that the college which combines liberal and vocational education has achieved the ultimate in the higher education of women. A recent study by R. G. Foster and P. P. Wilson entitled *Women After College,* the case histories of 100 women graduates of colleges, indicates all too clearly how inadequate colleges of all types have been in helping women to meet the problems which life after college has brought. The major areas in which these problems arise are family relationships, financial management, housekeeping, relations with associates, health, recreation, sex, and religion. The general conclusion of this important study is that there are certain inevitabilities in the lives of women that education has largely ignored.

I commend this study, as providing facts and points of view which must have increasing weight in any intelligent approach to the improvement of women's education.

Traditional versus Progressive Education

WHAT IS THE CONTROVERSY BE-
tween so-called progressive education and that which
it is supposed to displace?

I should make it clear at the outset that traditionalists
and progressives in American education are both striving
for the same ultimate goal: a free man in a free society.
The controversy between them arises over differences
in theory and practice as to *what* to teach and *how* to
teach to accomplish this end. In the interest of clarity,
I shall state the beliefs of each in such a manner as to
accentuate the differences. Actually I have yet to meet
a conservative school man who would agree that he
was a traditionalist, or one of progressive sympathies
who failed to explain that he was not a progressive with
a capital *P*.

The traditional school defines the goal of education
as preparation for adult life. It insists that there is a
common body of truth which is timeless and which must
be transmitted to the coming generation. The curriculum is an orderly arrangement of subjects which the
logical demands of the subject-matter control. The
educational process is one of discipline in the facts,
skills, and methods of thought that characterize the intellectual life. Certain subjects, notably the classical
languages and mathematics, are believed to be superior

vehicles for developing the human mind and will. The school knows what is good for the pupil and does its best to see that he gets it. Its effectiveness is judged by the extent and quality of the pupil's *knowledge* and by his ability to apply the principles learned.

The progressive school insists that education is not only preparation for living; it is part of the practice of living. It believes that the subject-matter of education must change with changing times and must vary with the social and personal needs of the learner. The educational process is not one of pouring in, but of drawing out the powers latent in the learner. Thus the curriculum is said to be child-centered instead of subject-centered. The progressive denies that there are intrinsic differences in the disciplinary values of subjects. Rather he maintains that material which is close to the life situations faced by each individual learner possesses the greatest developmental value for that learner. The progressive school judges its effectiveness by what the learner is *able to do,* and by the *attitudes* which he exhibits in his mental behavior.

This analysis is far from complete, but it will suffice to show that there are fundamental differences in the theory underlying traditional and progressive education. Now for some differences in practice.

In the traditional elementary school, the three R's form the backbone of the curriculum. The emphasis in teaching is on drill in these fundamentals. History, geography, and science are taught, but mainly to establish facts in the mind of the learner. In the traditional secondary school, the curriculum is dominated by the objective of college preparation, with its insistence on extensive study of mathematics and foreign language. The progressive school gives less time to drill in the three R's. It seeks rather to develop competence in the fundamentals through their use in materials drawn from literature, the social sciences, science, the arts, and contemporary life. In the progressive secondary school, academic studies are better related to the demands of modern life; and the social studies, fine arts and music, vocational education, and health education achieve a prominence far beyond that afforded to them by the traditional school. Under guidance, each learner selects a program which is appropriate for him.

Perhaps the greatest difference between the traditional and the progressive school is what might be called the educational climate in which the student works. The traditional school seeks conformity to established rules. The pupil is motivated in his learning by his desire to avoid the penalties attached to failure. The result is that unless he is interested, the quality of his effort and achievement is low. The progressive school maintains an informal atmosphere where the freedom of the student is limited only by the interests of the group as a whole. The teachers try to present educational situations in which the learner's known interests are appealed to, and to set the stage for his acquiring new interests on progressively higher levels. The student learns to be a good citizen as an adult by first becoming a good citizen in the school community.

As in most controversies, each party has some truth on its side. In my opinion, the progressives have the better theoretical argument, since their conception of education is based on the findings of modern psychology. In attempting to apply these findings, the progressives have sometimes lost all sense of balance and have been responsible for much of the superficiality of modern education. Nevertheless, the fears expressed by the traditionalists that the fundamentals would suffer in the progressive schools have not been realized. In the most authoritative study yet made, the graduates of progressive schools have shown that their possession of the abilities needed for intellectual pursuits in college is at least as good as that of graduates of traditional schools. On the other hand, occasional students who have not done well in progressive schools have transferred to traditional schools and found in their new environment greater realization of their capabilities and greater happiness. Because of our imperfect knowledge of what is best for the individual and what is best for American society, some children will undoubtedly be better off in one type of school than in the other. A good traditional school may serve well the needs of the few; a good progressive school will serve better the needs of the many.

If the time ever comes when educators agree on what the schools should teach and how they should teach it, I believe we shall find that the progressives have contributed more than the traditionalists to the evolution of the ideal school. But that time will never come. The American school system, like the nation as a whole, will always exhibit the clash between the traditional forces that make for stability and the progressive forces that make for growth. Each serves as a check on the other. Far from being puzzled by the conflicting claims of the traditionalists and the progressives, we should welcome them both and find in their co-existence the means for attaining higher standards of excellence in the nation's schools.

What College, If Any, for Your Son or Daughter?

A COLLEGE EDUCATION IS AN IN-valuable experience for many young men and women, but it is a mistake to assume that it is so for all. Going to college has become so much the habit of mind of the American people that we tend to close our eyes to the large number of young people for whom the college experience is harmful rather than helpful. To be successful in college a young man or woman must have high intelligence, social maturity, and a real purpose in life which the college of his choice can help him achieve. In advising parents about their own children, we can more easily say what not to do than what to do. Here are a few of the *don'ts:*

Don't bring a child up with the idea that of course he is going to college. He may not have the necessary ability, though you, his parents, are college graduates.

Don't send your son or daughter to college to play football, to make a fraternity, or to have a good time. He may do all of these things incidentally, but college work should be above all an intellectual experience.

Don't send your son or daughter to a certain college because you have sentiment about it. It may not serve his particular needs as well as some other.

Don't send your son or daughter to college unless you can finance the whole of the first year's expense and a substantial part of the rest. Although an occasional student has the brains, the stamina, and the opportunity to work his way through college, many break under the strain. Colleges do not have enough scholarships to aid all who are deserving, and hence reserve their funds for those who have proved their ability to do well.

Don't assume that your child's life is blighted or his education stopped if he doesn't go to college. The workaday world can provide a rich education to anyone who wants to learn, and the opportunities for adult education are legion.

On the positive side, I strongly urge your taking into account what the secondary school teachers and principals advise. Although they may make some mistakes in guidance, they frequently understand your child and his abilities better than you do, and they are more likely to know the varied college opportunities that exist.

But most important of all is the child himself. What intellectual interests does he possess? Does he work well with abstract ideas? Is he more interested in people than in things? Has he artistic or musical talent? What does he want to make of himself?

Although there are a lot of wrong answers to the question of what college, if any, is best for your son or daughter, there are several right answers. The variety of programs offered by colleges gives discerning parents, working with their sons and daughters and with the schools, a good chance to reach a wise decision.

Education for Citizenship

SOME PEOPLE THINK OF THE RE-
sponsibilities of citizenship as practically synonymous
with the exercise of the franchise on election day. According to this conception, our best citizens would be
those who "vote early and often"! Without in any sense
disparaging the efforts of those organizations which
focus attention on the act of casting the ballot or of
influencing desirable legislation, I should like to invite
attention to what I believe to be a more fundamental
conception of citizenship and one which if provided
through education will indirectly result in improved
political leadership and better legislation.

Education for citizenship means to me at least three
things: a growing understanding of the forces that influence group actions; an effort toward the elimination
of racial, political, and economic prejudices; and the
development of social conscience. If we would have
good citizenship, therefore, we must influence the individual's intellect, his emotions, and his will.

Most of our effort in educating for citizenship has in
the past been directed toward social understanding.
Thus we have courses in civics, history, and problems
of democracy in our secondary schools; and in history,
government, economics, sociology, and psychology in
our colleges. All of these aim to give the student an

intellectual perspective on the complex problems of society, if indeed they do not provide ready-made answers to these problems. Without entering into an elaborate discussion of the matter, we may fairly state that our schools and colleges are reasonably successful in laying a foundation of general understanding in these social sciences. I believe that the young men and women of today are far better informed on civic matters than their elders were at the same age, but I am not sure that they are better citizens.

The difficulty lies in the fact that the way people behave toward their fellows is only partly determined by how they *think* about social questions. How they *feel* toward these problems is much more important. Each of us acquired certain social, political, and economic prejudices in the process of growing up — prejudices which lead us to sympathize with the members of our own social group and to be apathetic or hostile toward those of different racial or cultural background. Education faces a difficult task in ridding us of these prejudices, because they are deeply rooted in emotion and astonishingly resistant to intellectual appraisal. The man who said he was a Democrat because his father was a Democrat and his grandfather was a Democrat, was simply more honest than most of us in admitting the part that *feeling* played in his political thinking.

If education is to produce better citizens, we must find a way to influence people's emotions and desires. To do this effectively we may need to employ the methods of the psychiatrist who delves into the individual's past in search of the experiences which produced his strong feelings and which account for his anti-social behavior. Once we have led students to recognize the sources of their prejudices, we shall have taken a big step toward removing them. The problem is one not only of knowing what good civic behavior is, but of associating satisfaction with actions which benefit the social group as a whole, and dissatisfaction with any other type of behavior. As long as people are proud of their prejudices, no progress can be made.

To my mind, therefore, our schools and colleges must give more thought to the education of the emotions, if a better citizenship is to result. It is of minor importance to "get out the vote" on election day, if the voter merely expresses the political prejudices of his group. As someone has well said, "The multiplication of error does not produce truth." Intelligent civic action will result not so much from a wider use of the franchise, as from a growing capacity on the part of the electorate to examine political issues dispassionately, in the light of a developed understanding and an increasing freedom from bias. The education of such an electorate is a task which will challenge our best efforts.

Why Educate Adults?

A SCHOOLBOY ONCE DEFINED AN adult as a person who had stopped growing at the top but kept on growing in the middle. Many of us would readily grant the latter part of this definition, and we can all think of acquaintances, presumably educated, who have ceased to expand their mental horizons. There is a widespread belief that youth is the period of life best suited to education. In adulthood our minds are thought to be less plastic, our perceptions less acute, and our memories less retentive. We admit, to be sure, that we have learned much by experience, and we are in the habit of thinking that our judgment is better. But all in all, we would hesitate to pit ourselves against youth in entering upon what would be for us a new field of learning. Yet the movement for adult education makes the rash assumption that "growth at the top" is not only desirable but possible, whatever our age.

Fortunately there is some scientific evidence in support of this assumption. Several years ago, Dr. Edward L. Thorndike, a professor of psychology at Columbia University, published in his book *Adult Learning* the results of his studies of the relative learning capacities of youths and adults. In his experiments, he compared both the speed of learning and the degree of achievement in groups ranging up to fifty years of age. The learning experiences included writing with the wrong hand, applying a code, typewriting, shorthand, Esperanto, and certain of the more formal high school studies, such as Latin and algebra.

In all his comparisons of learning ability, Thorndike found adults superior to children. He concluded that "in general, nobody under forty-five should restrain himself from trying to learn anything because of a belief or fear that he is too old to be able to learn it. Nor should he use that fear as an excuse for not learning anything which he ought to learn. If he fails in learning, inability due directly to age will very rarely, if ever, be the reason."

It appears then that the old adage "You can't teach an old dog new tricks," however valid it may be for dogs, is not true for human beings. But has Thorndike proved that you can teach an adult anything more than tricks? The studies he chose for his investigation were, in a sense, "trick" subjects. That is, they involved acquiring certain skills, remembering new facts, and applying relatively simple principles — abilities that could be readily tested. From his investigation we gain little knowledge of the capacity of adults to modify their habits of mind, their ways of living, or their sense of values, all of which are most difficult to measure. Yet it seems far more important to know whether adults can grow in these *basic* attitudes toward life than to discover that they can learn new tricks.

It is unfortunate that we have no adequate scientific evidence on the possibilities of improving the adult's more general patterns of behavior. Such evidence as we have suggests that fundamental changes in attitude are difficult to achieve. Yet the child-guidance clinics in our larger cities have been notably successful in redirecting the lives of certain delinquents, and the psychiatrists have helped many emotionally immature people to re-educate themselves to an adult level. It is a matter of common observation, however, that as adults we tend day by day to think the same thoughts, exhibit the same prejudices, accept our own way of life as best. But we need not conclude that such behavior is inevitable. We can adopt the more hopeful view which the evidence seems to support, that it is possible for adults to achieve better attitudes if they really desire to. We *can* learn if we *will*.

It is not clear then that the period of youth is better suited to education than the period of adulthood. Youth has the advantage that its attitudes are less fixed and hence more readily modifiable. But adulthood brings a deeper sense of purpose and provides a richer background of experience to make learning meaningful.

II

If for the purpose of our discussion we grant that adults can learn, does it follow that there is a clear need for a program of adult education? Our early efforts in this kind of education were directed toward the removal of illiteracy, the Americanization of foreigners, the extension of opportunities to those whose formal schooling had been prematurely terminated. None of these purposes is as valid today as it was a decade or two ago. Great gains have already been made in the removal of illiteracy, restricted immigration has reduced the need for teaching English and the rudiments of citizenship to foreigners, and the phenomenal growth of the public secondary school has extended substantially the period of schooling of the average child. Why, then, do we need adult education?

The necessity grows out of the total situation of which we are a part, and is accentuated by the general social unrest characterizing our times. We have witnessed, at first with awe and later with some misgiving, the scientific developments of our age — developments which have multiplied many times our productive capacity. Yet we find ourselves confronted by such phenomena as the concentration of the means of production in the hands of the few, widespread unemployment and poverty, crop surpluses, increased burdens of taxation, racketeering, increased incidence of mental disease, and bad housing. It is obvious that our social institutions have not evolved to the point where they are adequate to cope with these difficulties. The success of the attempts we are making or shall have to make in the future will depend to an extent on the efforts of the American people generally to understand the problems and the methods proposed for attacking them. Here is a need for adult education which is growing in importance with the passing of the years.

If our program of education for youth were more adequate to meet social and individual needs, the field of adult education would be more restricted than it is. But in spite of the gains made in formal education in recent times, it can hardly be said that the average product of our schools and colleges is broadly educated. We have pointed with pride to the increasing proportion of our population who have received the benefits of extended schooling, without examining too critically just what benefits this extended schooling has conferred.

Do the graduates of our secondary schools and colleges think and act in terms of an intelligent social philosophy? Have they rid themselves of the prejudices of the racial, religious, economic, and social groups from which they have sprung? Are they adequately prepared for marriage, for parenthood, and the responsibilities of family life? Has such preparation as they have received for earning a livelihood given them insight into the significance of the occupations they are to enter? Can it be truly said that our graduates have developed those intellectual and esthetic interests which provide resources for the enrichment of life? Do they possess the habit of independent thought? Are they flexible in their ways of thinking, feeling, and acting, so that they can adjust themselves easily to the changing conditions of life? Although education is striving valiantly to achieve the ends which these questions suggest, and although many graduates have made substantial progress toward these goals, it remains true that the average product of our schools and colleges is not ready to assume the responsibilities of adult living.

The causes of the inadequacy of our program for the education of youth are easier to state than to eliminate. Some are attributable to our failure to think straight about education, and hence are subject to change. Others present difficulties that are inherent in any program of education for youth.

We still suffer from the inherited doctrine that the best mental training is to be found in such subjects as mathematics and foreign languages, subjects remote from the experiences and interests of most students. Yet psychologists have not been able to discover that such subjects provide a superior discipline to those that have a more direct appeal. Again, many schools and teachers seem to think of education as a process of storing up knowledge, especially the lore of the past, without regard to the application this knowledge has to present problems. And students are encouraged to prolong their schooling on the ground that education pays in dollars and cents. The result is that the desire for economic and social preferment becomes for many the dominant motive for further study. Schools are also frequently handicapped by the unwillingness of patrons to permit discussion of controversial issues of our present life. Thus the very problems which concern us most are avoided as unfit subjects for the education of youth.

These are some of the forces which, to be sure, are subject to modification but which operate against the best interests of our schools. In time the counter-forces already at work will combat the evils and give us more adequate education. But there are at least two respects in which schools for youth will always be at a disadvantage in meeting our needs. In the first place, it is impossible to predict with accuracy the lines along which an individual life will develop. Times change and with them educational needs. The youth of today will live in the life of tomorrow. In some respects the educational demands of tomorrow will be different from those of today. In what respects, we cannot be sure. Hence we cannot plan a completely adequate program that concentrates its efforts on the early years of the youth's life.

Furthermore, schools for youth will always suffer disadvantage from the fact that youth has few responsibilities in the major fields of adult activity. Youth is denied the privilege of the ballot; marriage and family responsibilities are problems of the future; and entry into occupational life, at least for the majority, is postponed. Thus an education designed to prepare youth for adulthood will always lack the reality that attaches to similar education undertaken by adults.

The part that adult education can play in American life has become increasingly clear. We see that the need is not merely to provide educational opportunities for those to whom they have been denied in youth, but that there is work to be done in helping adults to solve their problems — problems which in large measure are the result of rapid social change and with which education for youth can never adequately cope.

III

If we ask ourselves what kinds of adult education promise most for society at the present time, our answer might properly assign the highest value to those which would help us understand the complicated social and economic problems of our collective life, those that would make us more social-minded in our thinking and acting. Next in importance we might name all that has to do with our education as consumers — the management of our homes, the care of our children both physically and psychologically, and the strengthening of our relationships within the family. Then we face the problems of our jobs. Adult education can enable us to increase our proficiency in our present tasks, prepare us for new occupations, and above all help us to find increased meaning in our work. Finally, there is the large field of personal cultivation, in which adult education can provide the means whereby we may extend and deepen our interests and resources.

All of these opportunities are significant for adult education. Although one can hardly be dogmatic about their relative importance, it seems that in the present state of unrest there is greater need for developing those forms of education which have social objectives than for fostering those which are more personal and individual in their aims. Up to the present, the courses which have drawn the largest following among adults have been courses for personal cultivation or vocational advancement. From the standpoint of numbers, courses designed to increase social understanding have proved less attractive. Is it not to be regretted that the strength of the popular demand seems to be inversely proportional to social need?

This disproportionate emphasis results, at least in part, from the fact that adult education has not yet reached the adult stage of its growth. Beginning as a series of unrelated efforts to meet particular needs, it has only recently become conscious of the necessity for a planned development. It has contented itself rather with providing for adults certain forms of education developed for youth.

In her admirable discussion of the broader side of adult education, *Adult Education and the Social Scene,* Dr. Katinsky draws a striking contrast between what adult education has been and what it must become:

"If education is to be adult education, it had better concern itself with things that adults must learn to do, rather than with spelling, Spanish, or a dilettante acquaintance with the classics.

"This does not mean that helping adults to acquire certain needed skills is an illegitimate function. But in and of itself it is not adult education; it is merely the teaching of skills to persons who are adults. It is not education at all, but merely training, unless it is integrated with the need of the person for it and the purposes for which he is to use it. To the extent that the purposes are those of the serious business of adult living, and to the extent that the person becomes more conscious, through his learning, of wider aspects of adult living, the process may become more truly adult education in a distinctive sense."

Whether conscious effort in the conduct of programs can bring adults to take a broader view of their problem remains to be seen. Unless it does so, adult education can expect to make only a limited contribution to society. Surely the task of attempting to make adults more intelligent planners of their own destinies is of vital importance. It is a task that demands our best efforts.

An Administrator's Dilemma

A Talk to the Faculty

A MEMBER OF THE FACULTY HAS asked me what attitude the Corporation takes toward the signing of petitions urging particular lines of political, economic, or social action. My answer is that I do not know, because there are so many shades of opinion in the Corporation. My guess is that if the question were put up to it, the Corporation would find itself in the dilemma of subscribing heartily to two propositions which are likely to come into conflict with each other:

1. That freedom of thought and expression must be guaranteed if democratic institutions are to survive, and that colleges must champion these rights.

2. That colleges today need friends as never before, and that nothing should occur which will place the College in an unfavorable light in the eyes of its friends, present or potential.

Hence the administrative dilemma: How to win friends and preserve academic freedom?

THE IMPORTANCE OF FRIENDS

Without, I trust, being an alarmist, I think I can say that the independent colleges are facing a period of great concern for their future existence.

1. Income from invested funds continues to decline; and in the face of higher corporation taxes to support the defense program, the returns from endowments may become so small as to make impossible the balancing of the College budget.

2. There is a general agreement that higher tuition fees will result in accelerating a movement of students away from the private colleges to the public institutions, and not be a source of larger revenues.

3. Large gifts for endowment to colleges have for the most part ceased, owing to steeply graduated income taxes and to the multiplication of deserving causes claiming financial support from people of means.

4. At the same time that these forces combine to reduce income, the need for increased expenditures is constantly before us.

5. Anything that happens which results in unfavorable publicity makes more difficult, if not impossible, the making of friends.

THE IMPORTANCE OF ACADEMIC FREEDOM

So much has been said and written on this subject that I can add little to it. My point of view may be summarized as follows:

1. Freedom of thought and expression are essential to a democratic society.

2. Colleges and universities must stand for the pursuit of truth wherever it leads.

3. College teaching should aim at the development of independent thinkers. Students can best be led to that level of thought by instructors who are themselves stimulating, independent thinkers, but who have a wide tolerance for points of view they do not accept.

4. Antagonism on the part of students towards the views of an instructor is evidence either of the teacher's

failure to keep his own emotions in check or of his failure to recognize the emotional immaturity of his students. In either case his success as a teacher is questionable.

5. College teachers have the rights of other citizens in the free expression of their ideas. When we speak on matters which are likely to arouse the public, it is a courtesy to the institution to point out that one is speaking as a private citizen.

6. Those of us who think of ourselves as liberals must especially guard against illiberality. I sometimes think that the most intolerant people in the world are the liberals. (If you object to my holding that belief, it is evidence that there is something in the idea.)

7. In times like these, when feeling runs high, it is important that in our dealings with each other we should be scrupulously careful to defend the other fellow's right to hold what we regard as a totally unsound idea.

8. I believe in academic freedom, and if the occasion arises, which I hope won't, I am prepared to defend before the Corporation the right of the members of this faculty to the free expression of their views.

THE DILEMMA

The proper answer to the question of signing petitions and publicizing results leaves me uncertain of what attitude I should take.

1. From the standpoint of winning friends, the publicity is bad in so far as it divides the public into those who applaud and those who denounce, even though a majority in the middle are not especially concerned.

2. From the standpoint of academic freedom, the College has no right to insist that only those ideas which it believes will win friends shall be publicized. It does not seem inappropriate, however, to request that faculty

and students use the established channels of the public relations offices whenever releases include the Simmons name. (This request concerns only *deliberate* efforts to use the name of the College in connection with publicizing ideas. Accidents are bound to occur, of course.)

3. The question of signing public petitions seems to me to be one which each faculty member must answer for himself.

4. Without in any sense attempting to influence the direction of that answer, but solely to contribute to the understanding of the problem by those of the faculty who have yet to find a satisfying answer, may I state the policy which I have adopted for myself?

(a) I recognize that the public is not interested in the views of Bancroft Beatley except, perhaps, on certain educational questions where he may be said to have an expert opinion. The public is very much interested in what college presidents, including the President of Simmons, think about all manner of public questions.

(b) I believe, therefore, that it is impossible for me to give my views publicly without their being identified in the public mind with the name of Simmons College.

(c) I recognize, furthermore, that on most public issues on which my opinion is sought, there are wide divergencies of opinion within the faculty, even among those best informed on the subject.

(d) Because I believe that I cannot dissociate myself as a citizen from myself as the President of Simmons in the public mind, and because I believe it important for the College to make new friends as well as to hold old ones, I attempt to limit my public pronouncements and endorsements to those questions on which I think I am adequately informed and on which my view, if interpreted as the view of the College, may do some good, and little, if any, harm. For example: I declined to endorse the William Allen White manifesto on aid to Britain, not because of lack of sympathy for the idea, but on the ground that I could not properly speak for the College. On the other hand, I endorsed the initiative petition on the birth-control question, because it had technical significance in at least two of our professional schools.

(e) In other words, although I insist that as a citizen I have the right to express my views, even foolish ones, I choose in what seems to me the best interests of the College to impose a censorship on myself.

5. The larger question of how the administration should resolve the dilemma is one which I find baffling, and I should appreciate any advice that any of you may want to give me. At present I can think of no better plan than to continue the consciously adopted laissez-faire policy and to hope that the members of this faculty will impose on themselves whatever restraints they individually believe are for the best interests of the College and the nation.

Part three

Simmons College After Fifty Years

CONTINUITY AND CHANGE: THESE are the opposing forces that shape us as a nation. In this we are not unique. All established societies owe their development to the interplay of continuity and change. Here in America, our particular genius for growth seems to lie in the speed with which we change to meet new circumstances and in the firmness with which we hold to fundamental values.

In no aspect of American life is this pattern of growth clearer than in our unsystematic system of higher education. No country rivals us in the diversity of our educational purposes or in the speed with which we adopt new programs to serve specialized interests. Yet one of the strongest educational forces of our times is the current concern for "general education." We hold firmly to our belief in a cultural tradition that is vital, whatever form specialization may take.

As we look back over a half-century of Simmons College, we note these two principles — continuity and change. From one standpoint, the Simmons of 1952 is so different from the Simmons of 1902 that it is hard to believe so much change could have taken place in a brief span of fifty years. Yet if we look beneath the surface to the basic ideas of the College, we see a continuity of purpose that makes the Simmons of today essentially like the Simmons of that earlier time.

Looking back to the scene upon which Simmons entered, we note that of the 25,000,000 women in this country in 1900, only 5,000,000, or one-fifth, were gainfully employed. Only one woman in every ten worked at a job requiring education beyond the high school, and most of these were teachers. Married woman workers were few, comprising only 5 percent of employed women. The great majority of women worked at unskilled or semi-skilled tasks in domestic service, manufacturing, or agriculture. Aside from the normal schools for the training of teachers and a few special schools for industrial or commercial training, there were not many systematic efforts to educate women for self-support. It is not too much to say that fifty years ago no institution of full collegiate grade was doing what Simmons set out to accomplish.

In this setting, Henry Lefavour, called upon to advise the Corporation of the newly-christened Simmons Female College, in 1901, urged upon them a concept of women prepared not for menial, unskilled, or semi-skilled pursuits, but for a higher level of competence, a higher degree of professionalism than was then thought suitable for women workers.

As most of my readers know, the College has often been thought of as concerned solely with technical education. This mistaken view is natural and perhaps inevitable since our acceptance of the professional objective is the chief feature that distinguishes us from other colleges for women. Yet even in our earliest beginnings the vocational was not thought to be the controlling purpose. For example, in his report for 1906-07, President Lefavour was careful to point out that of 130 courses offered, 69, or more than half, were non-technical in character. Today we attempt no such precise distinction between what is technical and what is not.

Yet we adhere steadfastly to President Lefavour's principle that both the vocational and the general are basic to Simmons thinking about women's education.

How was this principle first applied? By selecting at the outset three areas of women's work in which there was the prospect that the concept could be effectively demonstrated: household economics, secretarial studies, and library science. Almost at the same time, programs in general science and social work were started, but several years were to elapse before these enterprises attracted any substantial number of full-time students.

The second decade of the College witnessed the differentiation of the existing programs and experimentation in new areas. The School of Household Economics had already developed two specializations: dietetics and general home economics. In 1923, the School of General Science, hitherto somewhat indefinite in its aims, was recognized as having specific vocational purposes in chemistry, and in biology and public health. Between 1910 and 1918, the College extended its experimentation to four new areas: industrial teaching, salesmanship, public health nursing, and store-service education. Though both the School of Industrial Teaching and the School of Salesmanship proved to be short-lived, the undertakings in public health nursing and store-service education were successful and laid the foundations for our present School of Nursing and Prince School of Retailing.

Meanwhile, with all this growth and development, the balance between professional and general education was retained. We find in President Lefavour's reports of this period the hopeful observation that graduates seem to get jobs, to live useful lives, and to appreciate their training. It was not until 1917 that the evidence was unmistakable. Then, in the hurried mobilization for war, the demand for young women trained in technical pursuits was so overwhelming that the Faculty excused the majority of the seniors from their last month of classes and, waiving final examinations, granted them their degrees. Commenting on this turn of events, President Lefavour noted that "there has never been a more complete justification of the wisdom of the establishment of such an institution as this College."

He was able to be even more assured when, in 1920, he took the occasion of the twentieth anniversary of the first meeting of the Corporation to write a retrospect. Referring to the state of affairs at the founding of the College, he observed that "vocational education at that time was not recognized as a dignified effort of colleges." He went on to point out the adaptability of the basic concept of the College:

". . . [Simmons] has followed the development of the practical field by differentiating these various programs to meet special needs as they have arisen, always maintaining its policy of basing its technical work on a broad academic education. . . . Many of . . . [its] . . . graduates have themselves been pioneers in new fields and have by their initiative developed new vocations many women hereafter will follow."

It is unnecessary to trace in detail the changes in our educational offerings over the years. It is enough to note that the College has continued to meet new needs while preserving the idea of specialized preparation as a part of general education. Some of these new needs have found recognition in the establishment of a new school — for example, the School of Publication, in which industrial editing has become a major interest. Others have been met by the development of specialization within existing schools. For example, the School of Home Economics now offers a variety of specialties, among which child development, public health nutrition, textile analysis, and home economics education represent the more recent extensions of this program. The School of Business has added specialties in advertising, personnel, and medical records administration to its secretarial work and accounting. Similarly, physical therapy and orthoptics represent recent extensions of the offerings in the School of Science. These, together with parallel developments in the other schools of the College, have produced a diversity of opportunity that, so far as I know, is unmatched in the professional education of women.

Though the major divisions of our program have not increased greatly in number in the later years of our first half-century, there has been a startling change in the distribution of students within these divisions. Throughout our early history, the School of Business (then called Secretarial Studies) regularly provided half or more of the candidates for the bachelor's degree. That School, together with the School of Home Economics and the School of Library Science, accounted for about nine-tenths of our undergraduates. The remaining one-tenth was scattered over the Schools of Science, Social Work, Nursing, and other schools no longer a part of the program. Today, the distribution of students over the eight undergraduate programs is so even that no school provides more than one-sixth of the candidates for the bachelor's degree and every school presents groups of substantial size. This recent tendency of our students to spread themselves evenly over the entire range of our offerings reflects the wider and more diverse opportunities open to the educated woman of today.

Also noteworthy is the trend toward increased professional requirements in certain areas, which shows itself in the larger number of master's degrees awarded in recent years. Social work has become exclusively a field of graduate training. Librarianship increasingly demands graduate education at the master's level in preparation for professional types of work. Home economics education and public health nutrition are other areas requiring advanced levels of training, and nursing is tending in that direction for some of its more responsible positions. In contrast, we find that the field of retailing offers today more opportunities for undergraduates than formerly and that graduate education has become relatively less attractive to prospective students. Accordingly, our Prince School of Retailing, which, in an earlier period, was the largest source of candidates for the master's degree, is today dominantly, though not exclusively, an undergraduate enterprise. The College, by being sensitive to these modifications in the level of requirements, has again proved itself adaptable to changing conditions.

Up to this point I have reviewed fifty years of Simmons education primarily in terms of what has made the College unique: its sound principle of specialized education in a setting of general education and its capacity to apply that principle to the changing needs of the times. Though most of what I have said concerns the growth of the professional side of the College, you will quite properly conclude that our program has not remained static in general education. In common with other colleges and universities, our faculty is today more than ever concerned with finding the best way to transmit our cultural heritage, to enable our students to find meaning in life, and to provide a basic background of competence for all of life's activities. As have other colleges, we have focused more and more attention on the needs of the individual student as distinct from those of the group. Improved methods of selection, more intelligent educational and vocational guidance, better supervision of physical and mental health, increased freedom for self-direction in student life — all these and more serve to contrast the Simmons of today with that of the earlier years.

We can but be grateful for the rich heritage that is ours from those pioneer leaders of our distinguished past. Truly "they builded better than they knew." The scope of this address does not permit me to remind you of them by name. Though President Lefavour was responsible for defining the concept of the young college, he was ably abetted by Dean Arnold and a score of distinguished heads of departments who, with their colleagues of the faculty, interpreted the concept and applied it to their special fields. Today we acknowledge our debt to these early leaders and to those who succeeded them. We remember, in gratitude, too, those devoted members of the Corporation, the governing body, who as representatives of an interested public gave encouragement at every turn and whose successors today are an assurance of strength for the future. We salute, also, our forty-seven generations of graduates from the Class of 1906 to the Class of 1952, who, imbued with a sense of the significance of their education, are giving the best possible demonstration of the vitality of the Simmons idea by the way in which they are making their lives count for the common good.

And what of the future? What will Simmons College be like when it completes its one-hundredth year in 2002? Since none of us can see very far ahead, it is perhaps idle to speculate on the question. Yet we can find suggestions of our future by noting the direction of social changes now in process and the problems which these changes present. As the recent past has witnessed the extension of women's activities in science and technology, so the immediate future promises parallel opportunities in the social sciences. Simmons already has under consideration the establishment of an undergraduate School of Social Science to prepare young women for emergent positions in business, industry, and government, where the social sciences provide the technical equipment. As time goes on, other avenues will open, with the result that the distribution of professional interest among our graduates in 2002 may be as different from that of 1952 as today's varies from the pattern of our earlier years.

We see, also, in the social changes of our day a new relationship emerging between marriage and a career. Thirty years ago, the prevailing concept among women was a choice between the two. Today, more than one-quarter of all married women work. Compare this with the figure of 15 per cent before World War II and an almost negligible 5 per cent in 1900. In so far as college women are exhibiting this trend toward combining marriage and work — and there is nothing to indicate that they are not, — those of us who are concerned with the occupational education of women will need to find better ways than we have yet discovered for serving these dual objectives of job and marriage. Certainly there is little in the current scene to encourage us to devote increased attention to the vocational at the college level. Rather we should seek to reduce the technical requirements to the minimum consistent with initial success in professional work, thus allowing more opportunity for the study of home management and child guidance, leaving specialized forms of training to graduate levels of instruction, to be undertaken by those whose career motives have become more clearly established.

Another sign of the times is the evergrowing complexity of the social, economic, and political problems we face as a nation. As these problems become more pressing, we are more than ever persuaded that an intelligent, informed citizenry is needed to preserve our social well-being. This is a concern common to education at all levels. It presents both a difficulty and an opportunity to Simmons: a difficulty because so much time in the undergraduate program is necessarily committed to technical preparation; an opportunity, because of the possibility that we can apply this practicality, this functionalism of the Simmons concept to the problem of educating better citizens. It is not too much to hope that the establishment of a School of Social Science, far from diverting attention from this important area in the general education of all our students, will result in an increased impetus to civic education in the College as a whole, thus paralleling the impetus that our School of Home Economics gives to home and family life as an element of general education.

These, then, are some of the problems that lie ahead. They are new, and yet they are not new. They are different, and yet they are not different from those we faced at Simmons in the past. They are part and parcel of the continuity of the Simmons idea, as that idea finds new modes of expression to meet changed conditions.

In terms of a workable principle, Simmons has a rich inheritance. I think of no more fitting conclusion than to cite the final paragraph of President Lefavour's last report. Written upon his retirement in 1933, these words are equally appropriate today:

"We have now completed the foundation of the College. On it we may build a more perfect institution and increase its usefulness to the generations of students who will seek its service. The spirit of the past and the present are the assurance of the future."

ANOTHER LOOK AT WOMEN'S EDUCATION
Bevier Lecture, University of Illinois, 1950.

MARY JONES GOES TO COLLEGE
Simmons Review, *January, 1938.*

EDUCATION AND YOU YOUNG WOMEN
*Commencement Address, Radcliffe College,
Cambridge, June, 1950.*

THE COLLEGE OF TOMORROW
Simmons College Lecture, 1940.

THE COLLEGE AND VOCATIONAL EDUCATION
*Address, National League of Nursing Education,
Hotel Statler, Boston, May 11, 1937.*

THE FUTURE OF THE A.B. DEGREE
*Address, Massachusetts Division,
American Association of University Women,
Hotel Continental, Cambridge, November, 1942.*

TRADITIONAL VERSUS PROGRESSIVE EDUCATION
*Address, Third New England
War Conference Meeting
of Community Development Committee,
November 17, 1944.*

WHAT COLLEGE, IF ANY, FOR YOUR SON OR DAUGHTER?
Talk, Brockton Women's Club,
January 11, 1933.

EDUCATION FOR CITIZENSHIP
Article in Federation Topics,
Massachusetts State Federation of Women's Clubs,
February, 1939.

WHY EDUCATE ADULTS?
Substance of Address,
First Annual Banquet, Adult Education Center,
Twentieth Century Club,
Boston, May 3, 1934.

AN ADMINISTRATOR'S DILEMMA
Talk, Simmons College Faculty,
January 7, 1941.

SIMMONS COLLEGE AFTER FIFTY YEARS
Address at Simmons College Fiftieth Anniversary,
Symphony Hall,
Boston, November 6, 1952.

Date Due